An Introduction to Two Theories of
Social Anthropology

Methodology and History in Anthropology

General Editor: David Parkin, Director of the Institute of Social and
Cultural Anthropology, University of Oxford

AN INTRODUCTION TO
TWO THEORIES OF
SOCIAL ANTHROPOLOGY

DESCENT GROUPS AND MARRIAGE ALLIANCE

Louis Dumont

Edited and Translated by Robert Parkin

Berghahn Books
New York • Oxford

First published in 2006 by

Berghahn Books

www.berghahnbooks.com

© Robert Parkin 2006

Originally published in the series 'Les Textes Sociologiques', no. 6,
Paris etc.: École Pratique des Hautes Etudes and Mouton, 1971.

Second edition, 'Collection Tel', Paris: Gallimard, 1997.

Library of Congress Cataloging-in-Publication Data

Dumont, Louis, 1911-
   [Introduction à deux théories d'anthropologie sociale. English]
   An introduction to two theories of social anthropology : descent groups and
      marriage alliance / Louis Dumont ; edited and translated by Robert Parkin.
      p. cm. -- (Methodology & history in anthropology ; v. 12)
   Translation of: Introduction à deux théories d'anthropologie sociale.
   Includes bibliographical references and index.
   ISBN 1-84545-146-5 (alk. paper) -- ISBN 1-84545-147-3 (pbk.)
  1. Kinship--Philosophy. 2. Unilineal descent (Kinship) 3. Cross-cousin marriage.
4. Nuer (African people)--Kinship. I. Parkin, Robert, 1950- II. Title. III. Series:
Methodology and history in anthropology ; v. 12

GN487.D86 2006
  306.83--dc22

                    2005055852

British Library Cataloguing in Publication Data

A catalogue record for this book is available from the British Library

Printed in United States on acid-free paper
ISBN 1-84545-146-5 hardback
ISBN 1-84545-147-3 paperback

CONTENTS

EDITOR'S INTRODUCTION

I

Anthropology has generated an enormous number of studies of specific kinship systems, as well as theoretical disquisitions on kinship 'problems', but comparatively few general theoretical introductions to the subject for students. Things are a little better now than they used to be, with relatively recent books by Holy (1996), Parkin (1997a), Stone (1997, 2000) and Parkin and Stone (2004) to place alongside the old workhorse by Fox (1967) and the still unparalleled introduction for research students by Barnard and Good (1984). Among the very best of the earlier works is the present text by Louis Dumont, until now only available to readers of French. Basically it is an account of those two opposed, not to say hostile schools of thought known to anthropology as descent theory and alliance theory. It is a balanced and fair-minded account on the whole, though certainly not a neutral one, and the author's allegiance to the alliance theorists is plain throughout.

The text was originally written at the height of these debates, in the late 1960s. It therefore has historical significance with respect to a period when the intellectual foundations of the discipline were being keenly debated, even being developed to a large extent, making it highly suitable for inclusion in a series entitled Methodology and History in Anthropology. In addition, anthropology is currently experiencing a revival of kinship following its temporary eclipse in much of the 1980s and 1990s, and Dumont is still being invoked as a key thinker from an analytically more rigorous, pre-Schneiderian age (e.g. Carsten 2000: 4). It therefore seems opportune to bring this generally lucid and perceptive account of these debates before the anthropological public as a reminder of why kinship was and is so important to anthropology as one of the topics it has indubitably made its own, even though, for a period at least, it decided to experiment with dropping it almost entirely.

It is really for Dumont to give his own account of these debates in his own words, but some background to them may benefit the reader.

The conflict mentioned above between descent theory and alliance theory, which dominated post-Second World War anthropology up to the 1970s, involved a whole set of other oppositions. One was that, whereas descent theory became closely identified in practice with the anthropology of Africa, an area not generally associated with what Dumont calls 'positive marriage rules' (i.e. 'cross-cousin marriage'), alliance theory concerned initially Australia, as well as those parts of South and Southeast Asia where such rules are found with some frequency, though still far from exclusively. Another opposition was that, in initiating 'alliance theory' (the term itself is Dumont's) with his great but difficult work *Les structures élémentaires de la parenté* (1949), Claude Lévi-Strauss, Dumont's slightly senior contemporary, was opposing a French anthropological tradition to what had become a largely British one, though still with important French (specifically Durkheimian) roots. It was Radcliffe-Brown who was mainly responsible for this shift in British anthropology, which brought with it Durkheimian functionalism, as well as the substantialism with which Radcliffe-Brown and his followers are also associated. Lévi-Strauss developed Durkheimian ideas in another direction by applying Mauss's notion of exchange, which involves the idea of relation, to the problem of marriage, or more properly, affinal alliance. Dumont too was a follower of Mauss and like Lévi-Strauss a structuralist, if for different reasons (in Dumont's case, the discovery that structuralism explained his south Indian ethnography best, rather than any initial theoretical predisposition towards this particular approach). A further opposition between descent theory and alliance theory, therefore, was that between British functionalism and substantialism and French (later also British) structuralism. As Dumont shows, this is exemplified above all by the respective treatment of descent group exogamy in the two schools. For British functionalists and descent theorists, excepting A.R. Radcliffe-Brown to some extent, exogamy defines the descent group as a virtually self-contained entity. For French structuralists and alliance theorists, as well as their British followers, it is, by contrast, the key to relations between descent groups. These relations reflect the notion that exogamous descent groups (and not all descent groups are exogamous) cannot possibly be self-contained or independent of one another, since, in association with the incest taboo, their rule of exogamy forces them to obtain from other groups the wives they need for their own reproduction.

As hinted above, this opposition was not destined to remain a purely Anglo-French affair for long. In the 1950s and 1960s especially, these debates over kinship split British anthropology itself right down the middle, not to mention one particular department, Cambridge, where Meyer Fortes and Edmund Leach battled it out on opposite sides. At Oxford things remained more harmonious in this respect, for E.E. Evans-Pritchard, though a contemporary and life-long friend of the arch-descent theorist Fortes, had discovered a relational aspect to the Nuer descent system without having to bother with marriage very much at all. But as Dumont shows in these lectures, what Evans-Pritchard is describing is a structure of situations rather than one of a whole social and categorical system in the Lévi-Straussian sense. Also at Oxford, if a little later, Rodney Needham debated other aspects of the structuralist message with his one-time institutional colleague John Beattie (cf. Parkin 2003: 19–22). On matters of kinship, however, it was rather sniping from across the Atlantic that he had to contend with. This took the twin forms of Schefflerian substantialism (in intellectual alliance with the descent theorists; cf. Scheffler and Lounsbury 1971: 21–34) and a rejection of previous allegedly genealogy-based approaches in the form of Schneiderian scepticism (e.g. Schneider 1965).[1] Nor did the battle between fieldwork areas remain static. Asianists, Oceanists and Amazonianists were eventually followed by Africanists themselves in seeing 'Africanist' descent models as unhelpful. This culminated in Adam Kuper's debunking exercise (1982), which usefully reviews the history of what he calls 'lineage theory' at the expense of rejecting entirely the descent group model in anthropology.[2] Conversely, alliance theory has not swept the board either. Despite occasional apparent or phantom-like exceptions, elementary structures in Lévi-Strauss's sense cannot be seen as characteristic of areas like Africa, Europe, the Middle East, much of lowland Asia or upland South America.

As already indicated, since Dumont published these lectures in 1971, the study of kinship in anthropology has experienced considerable changes and competition from the rise of other topics to prominence, such as gender, personhood and the body. The latter especially has been significant in the context of anthropological treatment of the so-called 'new reproductive technologies'. The emergence of these technologies has had a lot to do with making kinship relevant again, although it is only tiny proportions even of western populations, let alone others, that exploit them. Whether attempts to combine or

---

[1] Actually, scepticism was a terrain that Needham frequently attempted to claim for himself: for example, like Schneider, if for rather different reasons, he also suggested that there was no such thing as kinship as a cross-cultural category (Needham 1971: 5).

[2] Kuper may have regarded this as a separate matter from the recognition of descent per se in indigenous communities: the latter is certainly more common than his dismissal of the associated anthropological model might suggest.

replace kinship with these other topics were ever satisfactory in either design or outcome is an open question. Certainly the period from the mid-1970s to the mid-1990s was a lean time for kinship, with deconstructive approaches, led by Schneider, reducing the earlier comparative and analytical aspect of kinship to almost zero in favour of an exclusive focus on indigenous, 'cultural' perspectives that, it was often felt, could not and should not be compared. As Anthony Good has pointed out on more than one occasion (Barnard and Good 1984: 178–80; Good 2000: 323–28), purely cultural accounts are themselves often open to criticism for their tendency to rely on one or a few informants, to miss variations in perspective within the culture as a consequence, to reify culture in a rigid manner, to reduce anthropology to ideology by ignoring practice or behaviour and the relationship of these to ideology, and to repudiate the comparative dimension in anthropology. Even as raw data, therefore, for Good such studies are frequently deficient.

Yet Good has not been alone in thinking that, at the very least, the cultural approaches initiated by Schneider's revisionism have over-reached themselves in deconstructing kinship as a largely western invention. Such comments come in part from scholars who are inclined to sympathise with Schneider's position as regards the alleged over-reliance on notions of genealogy, even biology, in earlier accounts of kinship. This neglects the fact that structuralism itself sought to undermine these notions in favour of category (see Parkin 1996; also the present editor's brief debate with Bouquet: Parkin 1997b, Bouquet 1997). Nonetheless, this shift suggests that it may now be possible to speak of a certain 'neo-Schneiderian' position, which accepts that kinship in some sense does exist – since otherwise human populations would not – but that it is not culturally represented in the same way everywhere. It seems to me that notions such as Carsten's 'relatedness' (2000) and Gavin's more explicitly neo-Schneiderien orders of 'sharing' and 'ratification' (2001: 118ff.) are attempts to establish some such position. However, as Holy has pointed out (1996: 168), invoking relatedness involves replacing kinship with a more nebulous idea that could, in principle, apply to any inter-human contact. Ironically, some varieties of structuralism – the archetype of formalism for the Scheiderians – also attempted to tackle this problem, resorting to the phrases 'relationship term' and 'relationship terminology' in order to get away from the genealogical implications of the words 'kin' and 'kinship' in 'kin term' and 'kinship terminology'. Yet 'relationship', like Carsten's 'relatedness', has a much wider reference than any notion of kinship, however broad and 'cultural' the latter may be.

At all events, since the mid-1990s there has been something of a revival in the formal side of kinship. Examples include Hage's prolific work (see 2001 and references therein), Read's mathematical approach (see 2001 and references therein) and the volume edited by Godelier et al. (1998). However, there have also been suggestions (which have largely remained such, it seems to me) from some neo-Schneiderians that a rapprochement ought to be sought between 'cultural' approaches and 'structuralist' formalism (cf. Carsten 2000: 4, who specifically mentioned Dumont as exemplary of the latter tendency). One should also mention the revival of approaches that seek to combine the strictly social sciences with psychology or biology, including the revival of sociobiology under other rubrics such as neo-evolutionism (cf. Hewlett 2001: 98). In other words, the traditional (despite Schneider's critique) emphasis that kinship is a social, not a biological matter is again being confronted by approaches that draw more heavily on the natural sciences. One difference at the present time, I would suggest, is that, in light of the new genetics, natural science approaches have become increasingly sophisticated in their methods, analysis of data and presentation of argument. There are also indications that the two sides are finding it more possible to cooperate than in the past, as is shown by the publication edited by Stone (2001) of the proceedings of a conference of the American Anthropological Association, which covers a variety of such perspectives. In engaging with such approaches in the future, social anthropology will surely have to resist glibly dismissing their proven or otherwise plausible findings while simultaneously continuing to insist that, for instance, whatever new genetic data might purport to show about the biological underpinning of social relationships, any society has at least some social obligations and kinship-like notions of relatedness that defy biology, or simply ignore it.

The fact that these debates were also being pursued in Dumont's time is a further reason for the continued relevance of his lectures. But not even this exhausts their interest for us at the present day. In the first place, as already indicated, Dumont played a significant part in the debates of that period, starting with his famous article on 'The Dravidian Kinship Terminology as an Expression of Marriage' of 1953, which perplexed and somewhat scandalised Radcliffe-Brown (see 1953); what Dumont has to say about those he opposed and supported is therefore of interest in its own right. Secondly, these lectures represent more or less the culmination of his thinking on kinship, since he did not publish much more than comments on his earlier work thereafter, often in the context of answering his critics (e.g. 1975; 1983: Chapter 4). Thirdly, in these lectures we see Dumont sketching out his thoughts on structuralism, the social sciences generally and hierarchy, all of which had recently played important parts in his synthetic account of Indian society, *Homo Hierarchicus* (1966; in

English 1972, 1980), and would continue to do so in his subsequent
work on western individualism and egalitarianism (e.g. 1986, 1994).
But finally, and by no means least, the lectures give an excellent
account of a field that still tends to perplex students, yet which is foundational for modern social anthropology, namely kinship as both
descent and alliance. It is hoped that their publication here in translation usefully and appropriately supplements their recent re-issue in
French.

II

In his preface to the published edition of these lectures, Dumont states
that his main aim in producing them is to introduce French students to
British social anthropology.[3] This aspect occupies the first two of the
three parts into which the published version is divided (broadly speaking, the first discusses what is meant by kinship, the second descent).
The structuralist approach of Lévi-Strauss on marriage alliance is
offered as something of a pendant in the third part, though it is actually
the longest of the three parts. Dumont stresses the necessity of clearly
distinguishing the two schools without ruling out their combination in
the future – something which has never really happened. He also points
out a further distinction, not coordinate with that between the two
schools but found in both of them, though particularly in Lévi-
Strauss's case, namely between restricted (scientific, systemic) theories
and general (metaphysical) theories. The problem of 'cognatic' systems
is mentioned, an idea which can apply to both theories, though in different ways (see further below). Dumont's additional 'personal commentaries', added to the published version but apparently not in the
original lectures, are justified as attempting to clarify difficult issues further, sometimes with the benefit of hindsight, but also containing his
own often substantial input into the ideas he has been discussing.
Dumont's bibliography lists separately what he has selected as core
texts, namely those he discusses in some detail, from supplementary
texts, which are merely passing references to confirm or refute some
particular point. This distinction has been retained here.

In Part I, which discusses what is meant by kinship, Dumont draws
attention to its traditional three aspects, namely descent, siblingship
and marriage, as well as the earlier conflation of kinship with consanguinity in England, as opposed to the regular inclusion of marriage
within *parenté* in France. Dumont also addresses the double meaning

---

[3] In this and the following section, I have not repeated references where these are provided by
Dumont himself in the main text: see his bibliography at the end of the text.

of French *filiation* (meaning both descent and the parent–child links which descent consists of; though it is relatively rare in English, the same word is used there in the latter sense only).

Radcliffe-Brown's idea of kinship is then discussed, since this is seen as foundational not only of the British school, but also of where it went wrong. Although Radcliffe-Brown sees kinship partly as the study of behaviour between individuals, he also treats it as a system or a structure that can be analysed. However, in Dumont's view, Radcliffe-Brown's wholes and structures are more a matter of juxtaposed elements than the ordered oppositions of Lévi-Straussian structuralism, not even Radcliffe-Brown's famous organic or functioning analogies being anything like the latter. Unlike in conventional British discourse, structure for Dumont is not a matter of the same trait possibly having different roles in different societies, for this would actually make it a different trait in the societies being compared. Dumont also rejects the notion that distinct sub-systems can be isolated in a social system (kinship, religion, economics, politics etc.), except sometimes as a useful first approximation. The comparison, between different societies, of sub-systems like 'kinship' systems is merely easier, not more real or cogent, than the comparison of whole social systems. This principle is based originally on Maussian holism and is important in most of Dumont's own work and that of his followers (e.g. Barraud et al. 1994; cf. Parkin 2003: Chapters 6, 7)

Another problem with the British school for Dumont is that functionalist approaches to kinship are based on the individual's place in the system, in the sense of his or her rights, duties and relations with, or behaviour towards, others. This is partly a legacy of Durkheimian sociology, which influenced Radcliffe-Brown profoundly and whose chief 'problem' was the embeddedness of the individual in society. For Dumont, this is 'sociocentric'[4] (or, as we would say, ethnocentric), principally because it fails to appreciate fully the importance of groups, especially descent groups, not in themselves but in respect of their relations (not behaviour here in the narrow sense) with one another. Indeed, for Dumont (and explicitly for functionalists like Fortes), functionalism has merely managed to reduce the descent group to the status of a corporate individual or 'moral person'. What is yet worse, this ethnocentric focus on the role of the individual, a clearly western notion here, easily slides into a discriminatory assumption that western kinship is the natural, standard, even superior representation of kinship in the world, of which all others are just

---

[4] This is not the only use of 'sociocentric' in the literature. For example, Allen (e.g. 1986) uses the term for what Dumont calls here 'global formulas of exchange', as opposed to 'local formulas', or what Allen calls the 'egocentric' perspective.

distortions. For Dumont, this is to let the side down, since in general he regards social anthropology as supreme in its ability to overcome ethnocentrism through its privileged knowledge and understanding, at once broader and deeper, of non-western forms of thought and representation. In this respect, it is superior to another leading social science, namely sociology.

Dumont's position here is also reflected in his treatment of the three-way debate between Gellner, Beattie and Schneider over whether kinship should be considered at least partly biological (Gellner) or more or less wholly social (Beattie) or cultural (Schneider). This drifted into another debate between Beattie and Schneider over whether kinship is merely a language or idiom doing no more than providing a form for content that is actually political, economic or religious in nature (Beattie), or whether it is itself content (Schneider). Dumont concedes Gellner's point that kinship involves biology at some level but stresses Lévi-Strauss's view that social anthropology is only interested in the extent to which different societies move away from this biological given and the various ways in which they do so. His support of Schneider against Beattie here, to the effect that kinship is certainly content and not mere form, receives further implicit expression later on (§18), when he asks whether the political dimension that Evans-Pritchard sees in the Nuer lineage system really requires the identification of a separate territorial system (and thus a 'political' one in its own right).

Dumont then turns to discussing the relative importance of kinship terminologies and behaviour, in other words Radcliffe-Brown's 'attitudes', in the thought of the two schools. Dumont stresses that, although Radcliffe-Brown rejected the use of kinship terminology to support speculative historical reconstructions in the work of W. H. R. Rivers and Lewis Henry Morgan, he also disagreed with Alfred Kroeber's position (1909) dismissing the social relevance of terminologies entirely, the latter being a position broadly similar to Bronisław Malinowski's dismissal of 'kinship algebra' in Britain. For Radcliffe-Brown, kinship terminologies were important expressions of the social structure, though in terms of descent at least as much as affinal alliance. However, he would not be followed in the attention he gave to terminologies in British anthropology until the arrival of Leach and Needham, and then they would shift the emphasis firmly away from descent and functionalism, and towards alliance and structuralism. In addition, Needham – who once boasted on a dust jacket (1974) that he had 'published more original work on kinship' than even Lévi-Strauss – completely rejected any relevance to the notion of Crow-Omaha systems (1971: 13–24), which were among those that had interested Radcliffe-Brown. This was partly because of what Needham considered the false correlation of such systems with unilineal descent, but also because they did not seem to constitute a single identifiable 'type'. However, long before either Needham or Lévi-Strauss had written a word on kinship, Radcliffe-Brown had also contributed significantly if not conclusively to the understanding of terminologies that expressed forms of affinal alliance in Australia (1930–1931). More generally in his work, in addition to the terminologies, he also emphasised behaviour and attitudes, exemplified most strongly in his studies of joking relationships, especially the avunculate (a privileged relationship between mother's brother and sister's son in certain societies). For Dumont, what is entirely characteristic of Radcliffe-Brown's account of this institution is that he manages to reduce it to a concealed aspect – hidden or historically redundant – of descent, using the argument that the avunculate represents a male ego's 'natural' affection for his mother that is transferred on to her brother. In that it also involves a clandestine if generalised psychology and a resort to evolutionary speculation, it goes clearly against Radcliffe-Brown's more general statements, especially the Durkheimian irreducibility of the social to anything outside itself. This tendency to reduce kinship to an aspect of individual relations and even attitudes in the British school is also found in both Fortes and Evans-Pritchard, who both firmly distinguished family from kinship in the sense of the lineage system (see further below).

Lévi-Strauss also addressed attitudes as part of his early, general refutation of functionalism. Dumont lumps him together with Radcliffe-Brown on the purely negative basis that neither of them studied kinship terminologies in isolation from other aspects of the social. However, unlike Radcliffe-Brown – who ultimately privileged descent, reduced kinship to it and started the trend in his followers to reduce even descent itself to mere property – Lévi-Strauss ultimately does not privilege any surface aspect of kinship over any other. For the structuralist, a structure is not simply a pattern of ordered oppositions, but an aspect of the unconscious side of common human mentality that underpins many conscious expressions that are equivalent (i.e. cannot be prioritized) among themselves. As far as kinship is concerned, behaviour is one of these expressions, the terminology another, the marriage system yet another.

In Part II, Dumont tackles the question of descent itself in more detail, discussing in particular the ambiguity in the French equivalent *filiation*, which, as we have seen, is used for both filiation as links between parents and children and the genealogically deeper chains of descent formed from them. His only real hero in this story is Rivers, who, around the turn of the twentieth century, had already clearly distinguished descent from succession, inheritance and residence as membership in unilineal, exogamous groups. Rivers also rejected cognatic groups as true descent groups because of their frequent lack of exogamy and therefore of clear boundaries, although as Dumont notes they are not central to the British school in this period (although Firth discussed them early on in Polynesia [1957, 1963], Leach a little later in Sri Lanka [1961a]). Dumont approves of Rivers's clarity in these respects and regards the whole subsequent history of British anthropology as a fatal deviation from it. Radcliffe-Brown himself quickly became more concerned with establishing descent as a matter of succession (to rights) in Rivers's terms, since both rights and duties transmitted by descent were important for an individual's personal status and position in society. Thus Radcliffe-Brown was both like and not like Rivers in this regard: in particular, marriage was still important to the former, just as descent groups had been defined by their exogamy for the latter. But as time went on – that is, between roughly 1924 and 1950 – Radcliffe-Brown's position gradually slid more and more into one of reducing descent to succession as defined above, and indeed, of confusing the two.

Here too, Dumont emphasises the unfortunate focus in the entire British school on the individual and his or her position in society, rather than on groups as constitutive of society, except in so far as these too appear as moral individuals. For Radcliffe-Brown and, following him, Fortes, the jural or legal aspect into which they inflated this concentration on the individual's rights and duties was explicitly important in all traditional societies, even though it was an essentially modern, western concept. Dumont contrasts this with his own ethnography on caste in India, which he saw as being formed around paired complementarities that were structuralist in character, not as virtually isolated groups reified as jural individuals with legal properties.

Dumont then turns to an examination of the work of Evans-Pritchard, one of his former colleagues from the years he spent in Oxford in the mid-1950s. This period gave him a greater insight into the British school than many of his French colleagues, as well as leaving its mark on his own thought. For Dumont, although Evans-Pritchard's work on Azande witchcraft (1937) established the principle of the relativity of ideas, it is his study of the Nuer (especially 1940) that is of most interest here. Although the focus on descent in the book, through its examination of the lineage and clan system, represents continuity with Radcliffe-Brown, the treatment of the system as political rather than jural represents a break with the latter. But what makes Evans-Pritchard something of a structuralist hero, or at least a structuralist *manqué*, for Dumont is the former's demonstration of the relativity of descent groups among the Nuer. This is because they only emerge as units of action in accordance with a process of segmentary fission and fusion, which itself depends on precisely where in the 'structure' conflicts between whole groups themselves or, at least as importantly, their segments are located. That is, while 'maximal' descent groups can in principle be conceived of as having outer boundaries, through exogamy once again, in day-to-day contexts of feuding and retaliation the units involved may well be smaller. It is explicitly the principle of lineage segmentation that both permits and produces this form of structural relativity. This is very different from Radcliffe-Brown's view of social structure (or in his own terms, the 'structural form' of a society; see 1952: 192), in which descent groups appear as rather static jural or legal entities, not as political actors assuming different forms through a segmentary principle. There is thus a clearer distinction between concept and action, ideal and real, in Evans-Pritchard's model. Another aspect of both structural relativity and the pragmatics of action comes from the fact that Nuer lineages and clans are in practice dispersed territorially, not entirely localised, as they tend to be for Radcliffe-Brown and particularly Fortes (and even Leach), despite their theoretical identification with particular territories.

Dumont also discusses at some length the relationships that Evans-Pritchard maps out for the Nuer between kinship (in the narrow sense of the family, but here including marriage), the lineage system and the territorial system (the latter being focused in the first instance on the different tribes into which the Nuer are divided). For Evans-Pritchard, kinship is important in being cognatic, not agnatic like the lineage system, since non-agnatic (uterine, affinal) relations are among those that underpin relations between different territories or localities. But also, says Dumont, in this view group relations necessarily require enduring groups, which kinship in Evans-Pritchard's narrow sense cannot provide, with the consequence that it cannot have, or be, a true structure. Although Evans-Pritchard's treatment of exogamy represents a partial return to Rivers, for him it links groups rather than defines them. Marriage itself is not seen as terribly important to Nuer except as regards bridewealth payments – a frequent source of disputes leading to fission.

Despite his shift away from Radcliffe-Brown, which is radical enough in its way, Evans-Pritchard has still failed to establish a true structuralism for Dumont, since he starts from groups and builds to the whole rather than vice versa, thus ultimately making relations between terms secondary to the terms themselves. Dumont hints that this comes from the very focus on politics in *The Nuer*, which in western thought is seen as a matter of power relations between groups (often, however, in the form of states) and individuals. It can also be pointed out that the structural dynamics of the Nuer case are mostly presented as being internal to a group of whatever size: it is therefore not a matter of formal and rather static relationships between groups through marriage, as for Lévi-Strauss. The appearance of the whole society as an actor in a conflict is therefore contingent for Evans-Pritchard, that is, dependent on the apparently rare context or situation where the Nuer as a whole are involved in conflict (e.g. against the Dinka, a neighbouring people). In Lévi-Strauss's case, conversely, as for Dumont, the whole society is always present and always one's starting point in any truly structuralist view.

Dumont spends some time showing the importance of myths as another way, besides non-cognatic kinship, of uniting Nuer groups that are otherwise separated by their exogamy. But his most radical comment on Evans-Pritchard's well-known account is to question whether the territorial system, which Evans-Pritchard represents as running in tandem with the lineage system, really exists as a separate form or principle of social organisation among the Nuer. This is basically because Dumont accepts Evans-Pritchard's claims for the existence of a lineage system as a mode of classifying, uniting and mobilising groups in Nuer society for particular ends, while including the political aspects of the system within these ends, which for Dumont do not need a territorial system in order to be pursued. In short, for Dumont, deleting territorial groups leaves one with a perfectly respectable lineage system which has political dimensions. This is diametrically opposed to those, like Ladislav Holy (1979a, 1979b) and Kuper (1982), who have questioned instead the existence of a lineage system among the Nuer on the basis that it does not correspond to the Nuer view of their own society. The main evidence for this is the problems that Evans-Pritchard clearly had at times in making the Nuer understand what he meant by a lineage.

The final chapter in Part II is devoted to discussing the development of descent theory in the hands of Meyer Fortes, a follower of Radcliffe-Brown in the main, and Jack Goody, a follower of Fortes. For Dumont, both figures grievously represent the reification of descent in substantialist terms in British anthropology and the final abandonment of Rivers' careful conceptual distinctions. Not only was Fortes concerned to establish an 'order of priorities' in the study of social institutions, with marriage coming way down the list, he also developed the notion of 'complementary filiation' as a way of reducing marriage virtually entirely to descent. This phrase was coined by Fortes to refer to the link of a child with the parent who does not carry the descent line in systems of unilineal descent. In particular for Fortes (given the patrilineal bias of his main ethnographic subject, the Tallensi of Ghana), this meant the mother where there was patrilineal descent. As Leach pointed out long before Dumont, Fortes uses this concept to argue that ego's ties of descent with his mother's brother (via his mother) are more important than the marriage that links the two groups of the mother's brother and the father through the transfer of a woman from one to the other. Again, therefore, we have an individual and substantialist perspective in place of the group-oriented, alliance-focused, structuralist perspective that Dumont prefers.

Like Evans-Pritchard, Fortes also distinguishes the lineage system from kinship in the narrower sense of the family. Just as Evans-Pritchard stressed non-agnatic as well as agnatic kinship at this level among the Nuer, so Fortes – and in agreement with the notion of complementary filiation – views filiation as basically bilateral, unlike descent. Similarly, just as for Evans-Pritchard the Nuer lineage system is largely about politics, so for Fortes the Tallensi lineage is the forum through which men conduct and control affairs in a political manner, though, in accordance with the influence of Radcliffe-Brown, for Fortes it is a jural even more than a political institution. The family, on the other hand, is the domestic group par excellence, an aspect of the 'web of kinship', whose role in governing relations between individuals is another factor making it distinct from the lineage system. Indeed, the web of kinship acts to integrate the lineage system against its own tendency to atomise itself because of the status the individual lineage assumes as a 'moral person'. This is contradictory for Dumont, because it is another example of the British disease of disregarding marriage as the real integrator of the whole society. Unlike Evans-Pritchard, Fortes emphasises the corporateness of lineages rather than their segmentation, thus making them even more a model of substance, not structure. Similarly, exogamy and marriage are treated as involving the transfer of rights over a woman from one lineage to another, not as group relations. Unlike Evans-Pritchard, Fortes lived long enough to answer at least some of his detractors; for example, he conceded nothing of substance in his reply to Andrew Anglin's critique (1979).

With Goody, the process described above goes a stage further and reaches its apotheosis in the insistence that descent groups are necessarily connected with the ownership and inheritance of property. This view is maintained even though Goody acknowledges that the property concerned may belong to the individual members of the group rather than the group itself and that what is 'owned' may be something intangible, like a myth or a ritual. For Goody, no other form of joint activity or organisation of a group is relevant, and he also ignores groups which are simply names and nothing else (Scheffler's 'descent categories'; see 1966). Dumont calls the single-minded apotheosis that British anthropology has arrived at with Goody 'Hegelian', though he might alternatively have said 'Marxist', given the focus on the nexus between property relations and social stratification that governs so much of Goody's work, then and since. It is clearly time, for Dumont, to leave this trend behind and examine, on the whole more fruitfully, a truly structuralist programme.

III

Dumont is clearly much more sympathetic to Lévi-Strauss and does not criticise him on fundamentals in the way he does the British school. However, he agrees with Lévi-Strauss's sterner critics that, great work though it is, *Les structures élémentaires de la parenté* often indulges in speculation based on misleading or poorly understood evidence. The work contains a restricted theory, dealing with what is conventionally called cross-cousin marriage (i.e. Lévi-Strauss's elementary structures), and a general theory, linking cross-cousin marriage with the incest taboo in a structuralist paradigm. Marriage alliance or affinity may appear to be as dominant here as descent is in the British school, but strictly speaking the two have equal standing and are complementary to one another. First, Lévi-Strauss's theory requires descent groups as the units between which affinal alliance is pursued, which does not always reflect ethnographic realities, as in the Amazon. Secondly, affinity does not 'become' consanguinity in the generations following the marriage, as it does in western societies and in the thought of the British school as regards the world in general. Indeed, given the manner in which cross-cousin marriage is repeated in each generation in any elementary structure, Dumont makes it clear that in effect it is inherited in a very real sense just as much as property or office may be. However, the reverse is not true, namely that descent is reducible to or 'becomes' affinity in course of time. Since African societies like the Nuer or Tallensi, which lack cross-cousin marriage, *ipso facto* lack the repeatable structure that goes along with it, affinity, though present, may indeed look very different than among the Kariera or Kachin (stock examples of different forms of elementary structure). Neither Dumont nor Lévi-Strauss, therefore, can ultimately reduce all 'tribal' social structures to their alliance-focused 'type' any more than the British school could to their descent-oriented one.

What Dumont calls Lévi-Strauss's 'restricted theory' is an explanation of the different 'types' of cross-cousin marriage per se (see below). For a full account, one requires the 'general theory', which links cross-cousin marriage to the incest taboo. The latter, for Lévi-Strauss, is part nature, part culture, and thus links them, as in myths explaining the origins of society through the abandonment of an earlier practice of incest. Lévi-Strauss does not, of course, treat such myths as actual history but as collective representations posing and then resolving the conundrums of human existence. In the present context, incest taboos are important because they force men to exchange their sisters for other men's sisters in marriage. Through marriage, in other words, one's sisters become other men's wives, and those other men become one's brothers-in-law. The latter shift is equally important, especially for Dumont, who had earlier described affinity as a matter of same-sex relations only (1983 [1953]: 21). In many societies with elementary structures in particular, brothers-in-law – who are also ipso facto classificatory male cross cousins – are key partners in other sorts of exchange as well.

But it is typically not just individuals who are involved in exchanges in elementary structures but whole groups. Affinal alliance is therefore an example of the 'total reciprocity' of Mauss – another source of inspiration for both Lévi-Strauss and Dumont. The avoidance of incest too can be considered a group affair in many societies with elementary structures (e.g. with marriage moieties or marriage classes; see below). By contrast, suggests Dumont, the British school can really only explain incest psychologically, not sociologically, because of its reduction of kinship to consanguinity and its neglect of the significance of marriage and affinity as the means whereby incest is avoided. In addition, Dumont could have stressed here again the focus on the individual in the British school, Evans-Pritchard aside to some extent. This led those in this school who did engage seriously with cross-cousin marriage, like Radcliffe-Brown, to link it with the rights and duties of the individual rather than the dynamics of group relations. Thus in this view, male ego has a claim on (i.e. a right to) his mother's brother's daughter as a wife. For most alliance theorists, indeed, the very expression 'mother's brother's daughter' indicates an approach relying on consanguinity rather than affinity, genealogy rather than category, individual status rather than group relations: it, and others like it, are therefore to be avoided.

There is, of course, more than one 'type' of cross-cousin marriage or elementary structure. This was known already long before Lévi-Strauss, Fortune's brief note of 1933 often being cited, despite its unconventional language, as the classic reference laying out the three formal types of cross-cousin marriage – bilateral, matrilateral and patrilateral – for the first time. For Lévi-Strauss, these become respectively restricted exchange, generalised exchange and a sort of mixed form. The model of restricted exchange, though not always its ethnographic reality, is one of immediate, direct exchange between any two groups. For Lévi-Strauss, it therefore has less integrative potential than generalised exchange, which involves indirect exchange between any number of groups from three upwards within a single system of

exchange. However, this makes generalised exchange more speculative, since one can never be sure that one is going to receive a woman
in return for one previously given. By definition in generalised
exchange, she cannot come from the same group (wife-takers are
always distinguished from wife-givers in this case). Generalised
exchange is also associated with the idea of 'marriage in circle', which
Dumont, following Leach and others, regards with scepticism. This is
apparently because he regards as transitive the hierarchical differences between groups that stem from the apparently invariant distinction between wife-takers and wife-givers, in which the latter are
usually superior – i.e. there is hypogamy in these cases, not hypergamy,
as Lévi-Strauss had thought. This leads Dumont to object that, if the
system turned back on itself in a cyclical fashion, it would conflict
impossibly with the hierarchy. In fact, the status differences involved
are usually purely a matter of relations between the two groups
engaged in the individual alliance and are therefore intransitive across
the whole system (cf. Parkin 1990). But Dumont also criticises Needham's study of the Purum on similar grounds as a 'gratuitous' demonstration of the existence of an astonishing number of marriage circles
for a population of a mere three hundred or so. Disregarding Needham's evidence, Dumont claims that there need to be fewer circles and
that they need to be present in the minds of the people – i.e. they
should be part of a 'global' formula – to be meaningful. In fact,
Lehmann showed that their existence was perfectly capable of surprising those embedded in them (1963). But still, for Dumont, the fact
that it is always possible to identify them locally, since 'each
"exchange" unit can see a circle closing in on itself', is not itself relevant. Here he is in effect blaming Needham, rather unfairly, for failing
to observe a distinction that Dumont himself has introduced.

Dumont is more in agreement with Needham's own scepticism
regarding the existence of patrilateral cross-cousin marriage as a separate form, but he remarks that this may still be how the people themselves view their system, as in south India, where individual families
keep track of who owes a woman to whom in all their affinal
exchanges. However, this is probably the case for all forms of cross-
cousin marriage. This does not affect the apparent finding that, at the
model level, there are no systems (as opposed to single instances) of
patrilateral alliance, and that indigenous explanations supporting the
assumption that there are are in reality nothing more than part of the
context in which fundamentally bilateral (direct exchange) systems
work on the ground.

Another distinction made by Dumont, again within the broad category of elementary structures, is between 'global' and 'local' formulas. The key difference here is the presence or absence of groups that

themselves express affinal relations of exchange. The simplest example is a vertical division of the whole society into two intermarrying moieties, in which one's own, non-marriageable group is distinguished from the group of one's affines (the only group into which one may marry). Another example is the Kariera of Australia, described in detail here by Dumont (see also 1983: Chapter 5), which are divided into four marriage classes: each moiety in the former system is divided further into groups of alternating generations, in such a way that ego can only marry into one marriage class. For the alliance theorist, such groups are not the same as descent groups, even where these govern marriage in their own way through their exogamy, though they may well have a patrilineal or matrilineal bias.

Dumont's systems with 'local' formulas lack groups like moieties or marriage classes, though they may have exogamous descent groups as described above. His stock example is south India, where he himself worked. The lack of groups creates a dependence on kin terms as a guide to whom one may marry, which seems at first sight to reproduce the individual focus of the descent theorists. However, in alliance theory cross-cousins are always 'classificatory', implicitly if not explicitly, meaning that category takes the place of genealogy – another key principle of alliance theory (cf. Parkin 1996). Thus there is also something collective involved, whether this is a group as with global formulas or a category as with local ones.

Dumont also discusses the relevance of descent in these systems from the point of view of what Lévi-Strauss calls 'harmonic' and 'disharmonic' regimes, that is, respectively systems where the rule of descent (patrilineal or matrilineal) and the rule of residence (patrilocal or matrilocal) are or are not in the same line. This recalls an earlier theory that systems of cross-cousin marriage could be explained through the interaction of the two theoretical lines of unilineal descent: while parallel cousins are linked to ego through one or other such line and therefore excluded by the rule of exogamy, cross cousins are not linked by either and so can be married. Dumont had already dismissed this argument (1983 [1966]: Chapter 6) as a further, extreme example of the reduction of marriage to descent by descent theorists, not least because in practice many of these descent lines had no meaning for the indigenous people concerned and could therefore only be considered 'implicit'. It is nonetheless possible to see them reoccurring in Lévi-Strauss's work in revised form, but what is really at issue here is how Lévi-Strauss links these two regimes to the two main types of elementary structure, disharmonic regimes being connected with restricted exchange, harmonic regimes with generalised exchange. However, while most of the latter probably are harmonic in practice, as Dumont points out the Kariera cannot be fitted into this paradigm, since they have a combination of harmonic regime (patri-lineal and patrilocal) with restricted exchange. These regimes also depend on a strict adherence to Rivers's definition of descent, some-thing Lévi-Strauss is not entirely consistent over. It must be said that few even of Lévi-Strauss's followers have made much of these regimes, which, however ethnographically accurate they may or may not be, do not help much in understanding how elementary structures them-selves work.

Dumont also stresses Lévi-Strauss's return to the study of the kin-ship terminologies in *Les structures élémentaires de la parenté*, a shift from both the latter's earlier position underplaying their significance as an object of study separate from other social institutions,[5] and the British school in the period between Rivers (or at least Radcliffe-Brown) and Leach and Needham. The latter two receive more promi-nence in the final chapter as key British supporters of Lévi-Strauss, though Leach had clearly anticipated his French colleague in his early fieldwork-based publications on the Kachin system and disagreed rad-ically with Lévi-Strauss over how it should be interpreted (Leach 1961b [1951]: Chapter 3, especially pp. 76–80).

Although Leach took it upon himself to introduce Lévi-Strauss to Anglo-Saxon anthropology, he was never wholly a structuralist and retained much functionalism in his own thought. One aspect of this, as Dumont points out, is the influence over him of Radcliffe-Brown's view of kinship as in part a matter of the study of behaviour. He also had a different view of the 'local' from Dumont, his 'local descent group' (Leach 1961b: 81ff.) being the local representative of the wider category (e.g. the actual spouse-exchange group rather than the exog-amous group as a whole), not the absence of distinct affinal exchange groups like marriage classes. Leach is also credited with correcting Lévi-Strauss over the latter's assumption that the status differences involved in generalised exchange were hypergamous, not, as is usual, hypogamous (see above). Leach also modified Lévi-Strauss's view of generalised exchange by reinterpreting it as a matter of the exchange of women against goods, not of women against women, as is more obviously the case with restricted exchange. However, both Leach and Dumont can be criticised for denying, in accordance with their respec-tive rejections of the possibility of marriage in a circle, that such status differences can derive purely from individual marriages. One begins to suspect at this point that, although Dumont was perfectly familiar with restricted exchange from his own fieldwork in south India, he

---

[5] Dumont does not specify the article in which Lévi-Strauss had adopted this earlier position, but it is presumably 'Structural Analysis in Linguistics and Anthropology', originally pub-lished in French in the journal *Word* in 1945 (see Lévi-Strauss 1963: Chapter 2).

was less aware of the finer points of generalised exchange. He seems to have followed Leach too closely here, not realising that the latter's interpretation of his own data is occasionally suspect and that not all examples of generalised exchange are exactly like the Kachin. In particular, most seem to lack the separate hierarchical, chiefly structure, transitive in kind, that one finds among the Kachin, Leach's own treatment of which I myself have contested elsewhere (Parkin 1990).

As already indicated, Dumont is much less sympathetic to Needham's work on these issues. Alluding to Needham's criticism of Lévi-Strauss for failing to distinguish properly between what Needham calls prescription and preference, Dumont raises the problem of the relationship between model and reality, asking what happens when the two appear to conflict because there is no 'cross cousin' available for a given ego to marry. His answer is the entirely standard one of invoking the classificatory principle: that is, as already indicated, even at the local level we are still dealing with something collective, namely a category, not an individual cross cousin, but nor with a group, very possibly, in the sense of those found in Dumont's 'global' formulas. This increases the possibility that a suitable spouse can be found for any ego, even where a genealogical cross cousin is lacking. Dumont therefore finds Lévi-Strauss's alternative distinction between mechanical and statistical models sufficient. Needham himself was later (1973) to add the latter as a third aspect, while transferring prescription from the level of rules to being a characteristic of the terminology. But here, some years before Needham published this well-known article, Dumont is already dismissing Needham's treatment of prescription as 'complex and draconian', and as characterising a type of system of which maximum analytical rigour is to be expected, not a description of a simple rule of cross-cousin marriage. For Dumont, this leads Needham to neglect a lot that passes for cross-cousin marriage, though this is to disregard Needham's comparison (1966–1967 – dedicated to Dumont, ironically enough) of the very different Garo, Manggarai and Mapuche examples of 'MBD' (mother's brother's daughter) marriage. Here, therefore, Dumont tends to dismiss Needham's distinction between prescription and preference, though elsewhere in the present text (especially in note 20) he sees a use for it. In south India, for example, it helps explain the co-existence of a regional model of restricted exchange with the unilateral preferences pursued by many local groups. It took a much later article by Anthony Good (1981) to demonstrate clearly how this sort of situation works in one south Indian sub-caste.

Dumont also notes that, while Lévi-Strauss had prioritised reciprocity, direct or indirect, between groups, Needham reduces this, as well as exchange, to opposition, this being a more general idea not necessarily involving the actual transfer of anything, though still being structuralist. Dumont himself points out that not all systems of affinal alliance are based on notions of exchange, which so much of the world has moved away from, though other aspects of kinship will always be important. For example, this is probably how one should interpret cognatic systems, which Lévi-Strauss regards as linking 'kinship in the proper sense' with 'the exercise of rights over the soil' (Dumont's words). However, Dumont concludes his account at this point, since this is work for the future (of which little if anything has actually been carried out).

IV

The present version of this translation is based on the second, Gallimard edition of 1997, though in making the final revisions the earlier Mouton edition of 1971 has been consulted, principally to help clarify a handful of obvious and easily corrected errors in the later edition (not indicated here).

The task of any translation is obviously to render the meaning of the original as exactly as possible in the target language, while making the latter read smoothly and naturally. In addition to attempting to follow these aims here, I have sometimes been compelled to go a little beyond these guidelines in rewording Dumont's prose where the construction of some of his explanations of English terms for a French readership would have produced a redundancy in the English version; I have not indicated this specifically in the text. I have occasionally used square brackets to give the French equivalent of an English term where there might be dispute or uncertainty in the reader's mind over what is meant. Some of Dumont's longer paragraphs have been divided at strategic points to make them more manageable. I have also retained the difference in type size used in the original.

I have generally translated *anglais(e)* as 'British' except where used of the language. I have checked and, where necessary, corrected Dumont's quotations from English-language texts. I have invariably used already published English translations of French texts by Lévi-Strauss where these exist. In these cases, two page numbers are given, the first relating to the French original, the second to the published English version. Dumont only lists 'basic works' in the bibliography in the original. I have retained this list, its order and presentation, but have added a second list of the other works he refers to in the order of their appearance.

I am most grateful to Dr Anne de Sales and Dr N.J. Allen for their advice on aspects of the translation and on Dumont's sometimes tortuous prose. I would also like to thank Dumont's widow and Galli-mard, the current rights holders, for permission to publish the present translation; Marion Berghahn, of the publishers Berghahn, for agreeing to undertake the work; and Prof. David Parkin, of the Institute of Social and Cultural Anthropology, University of Oxford, for agreeing to include it in the series Methodology and History in Anthropology, of which he is editor.

Robert Parkin
Oxford, July 2005

REFERENCES

Allen, N.J. 1986. 'Tetradic Theory: An Approach to Kinship', *Journal of the Anthropological Society of Oxford*, Vol. 17/2: 87–109.

Anglin, Andrew 1979. 'Analytical Models and Folk Models: The Tallensi Case', in Ladislav Holy (ed.), *Segmentary Lineage Systems Reconsidered*, Belfast: The Queen's University Papers in Social Anthropology, Vol. 4: 49–67.

Barnard, Alan and Anthony Good 1984. *Research Practices in the Study of Kinship*, London: Academic Press.

Barraud, Cécile, Daniel de Coppet, André Iteanu and Raymond Jamous 1994 [1984]. *Of Relations and the Dead: Four Societies Viewed from the Angle of their Exchanges*, Oxford: Berg.

Bouquet, Mary 1997. 'Kinship with Trees [correspondence]', *Journal of the Royal Anthropological Institute* (n.s.), Vol. 3/2: 375–76.

Carsten, Janet (ed.) 2000. 'Introduction: Cultures of Relatedness', in *Cultures of Relatedness: New Approaches to the Study of Kinship*, Cambridge: Cambridge University Press.

Dumont, Louis 1975. 'Terminology and Prestations Revisited', *Contributions to Indian Sociology* (n.s.), Vol. 9/2: 197–215.

_____ 1980 [1966, 1972]. *Homo Hierarchicus: The Caste System and its Implications*, Chicago and London: The University of Chicago Press.

_____ 1983. *Affinity as a Value: Marriage Alliance in South India, with Comparative Essays on Australia*, Chicago and London: The University of Chicago Press.

_____ 1986. *Essays on Individualism: Modern Anthropology in Ideological Perspective*, Chicago and London: The University of Chicago Press.

_____ 1994 [1991]. *German Ideology: From France to Germany and Back*, Chicago and London: The University of Chicago Press.

Evans-Pritchard, E.E. 1937. *Witchcraft, Oracles and Magic among the Azande*, Oxford: Clarendon Press.

Firth, Raymond 1957. 'A Note on Descent Groups in Polynesia', *Man*, Vol. 57: 4–8.

_____ 1963. 'Bilateral Descent Groups: An Operational Viewpoint', in Isaac Schapera (ed.), *Studies in Kinship and Marriage Dedicated to Brenda Seligman on her 80th Birthday*, London: Royal Anthropological Institute.

Fortune, Reo 1933. 'A Note on Some Forms of Kinship Structure', *Oceania*, Vol. 4: 1–9.

Fox, Robin 1967. *Kinship and Marriage*, Harmondsworth: Penguin Books.

Gavin, Kathy-Lee 2001. 'Schneider Revisited: Sharing and Ratification in the Construction of Kinship', in Linda Stone (ed.), *New Directions in Anthropological Kinship*, Lanham: Rowman & Littlefield.

Godelier, Maurice, Thomas R. Trautmann and Franklin Tjon Sie Fat (eds) 1998, *Transformations of Kinship*, Washington and London: Smithsonian Institution Press.

Good, Anthony 1981. 'Prescription, Preference and Practice: Marriage Patterns among the Kondaiyankottai Maravar of South India', *Man* (n.s.), Vol. 16/1: 108–29.

_____ 2000. 'Power and Fertility: Divine Kinship in South India', in Monika Böck and Aparna Rao (eds), *Culture, Creation and Procreation: Concepts of Kinship in South Asian Practice*, New York and Oxford: Berghahn Books.

Hage, Per 2001. 'Marking Theory and Kinship Analysis: Cross-Cultural and Historical Applications', *Anthropological Theory*, Vol. 1/2: 197–212.

Hewlett, Barry S. 2001. 'Neoevolutionary Approaches to Human Kinship', in Linda Stone (ed.), *New Directions in Anthropological Kinship*, Lanham: Rowman & Littlefield.

Holy, Ladislav 1979a. 'The Segmentary Lineage Structure and its Essential Status', in Ladislav Holy (ed.), *Segmentary Lineage Systems Reconsidered*, Belfast: The Queen's University Papers in Social Anthropology, Vol. 4: 1–22.

_____ 1979b. 'Nuer Politics', in Ladislav Holy (ed.), *Segmentary Lineage Systems Reconsidered*, Belfast: The Queen's University Papers in Social Anthropology, Vol. 4: 23–48.

_____ 1996. *Anthropological Perspectives on Kinship*, London and Chicago: Pluto Press.

Kroeber, Alfred 1909. 'Classificatory Systems of Relationship', *Journal of the Royal Anthropological Institute*, Vol. 39: 77–84.

Kuper, Adam 1982. 'Lineage Theory: A Brief Retrospect', *Annual Review of Anthropology* Vol. 11: 71–95.

Leach, E.R. 1961a. *Pul Eliya: A Village in Ceylon: A Study of Land Tenure and Kinship*, Cambridge: Cambridge University Press.

_____ 1961b. *Rethinking Anthropology*, London: The Athlone Press, and New York: Humanities Press (London School of Economics Monographs on Social Anthropology, 22).

Lehmann, Frank 1963. *The Structure of Chin Society*, Urbana: University of Illinois Press.

Lévi-Strauss, Claude 1949. *Les structures élémentaires de la parenté*, Paris: Presses Universitaires de France.

_____ 1963. *Structural Anthropology*, New York: Basic Books.

Needham, Rodney 1966–67. 'Terminology and Alliance I and II', *Sociologus* Vol. 16/2: 141–57, and Vol. 17/1: 39–53.

_____ 1971. 'Remarks on the Analysis of Kinship and Marriage', in Rodney Needham (ed.), *Rethinking Kinship and Marriage*, London: Tavistock Publications (ASA Monographs, 11).

_____ 1973. 'Prescription', *Oceania*, Vol. 42: 166–81.

_____ 1974. *Remarks and Inventions: Skeptical Essays about Kinship*, London: Tavistock Publications.

Parkin, Robert 1990. 'Ladders and Circles: Affinal Alliance and the Problem of Hierarchy', *Man* (n.s.), Vol. 25/3: 472–88.

_____ 1996. 'Genealogy and Category: An Operational View', *L'Homme*, Vol. 139: 85–106.

_____ 1997a. *Kinship: An Introduction to Basic Concepts*, Oxford and Malden: Blackwell.

_____ 1997b. 'Kinship with Trees [correspondence]', *Journal of the Royal Anthropological Institute* (n.s.), Vol. 3/2: 374–75.

_____ 2003. *Louis Dumont and Hierarchical Opposition*, New York and Oxford: Berghahn (Methodology and History in Anthropology, Vol. 9).

Parkin, Robert and Linda Stone (eds) 2004. *Kinship and Family: An Anthropological Reader*, Oxford and Malden: Blackwell.

Radcliffe-Brown, A.R. 1930–31. 'The Social Organization of Australian Tribes', *Oceania*, Vol. 1: 34–63, 204–46, 426–56.

_____ 1952. *Structure and Function in Primitive Societies: Essays and Addresses*, London: Cohen & West.

_____ 1953. 'Dravidian Kinship Terminology', *Man*, Vol. 53, 112.

Read, Dwight 2001. 'Formal Analysis of Kinship Terminologies and its Relationship to What Constitutes Kinship', *Anthropological Theory*, Vol. 1/2: 239–67.

Scheffler, Harold 1966. 'Ancestor Worship in Anthropology: or, Observations on Descent and Descent Groups', *Current Anthropology*, 7: 541–51.

Scheffler, Harold and Floyd G. Lounsbury 1971. *A Study of Kinship Semantics: The Siriono Kinship System*, Englewood Cliffs: Prentice Hall.

Schneider, David 1965. 'Some Muddles in the Models: or, How the System Really Works', in Michael Banton (ed.), *The Relevance of Models for Social Anthropology*, London: Tavistock Publications (ASA Monographs, 1).

Stone, Linda 1997. *Kinship and Gender: An Introduction*, Boulder and Oxford: Westview Press.

_____ 2000. *Kinship and Gender: An Introduction* (2nd edn.), Boulder and Oxford: Westview Press.

_____ (ed.) 2001. *New Directions in Anthropological Kinship*, Lanham: Rowman & Littlefield.

PREFACE

The present text is the result of a series of lectures given at EPRASS[1] (anthropology) in 1965–1966 and 1966–1967. In view of the lack of textbooks for the teaching of social anthropology in France, I had intended at the time to improve and complete this account with a view to its publication. But I have not had the time to carry out such a revision, and if this text now sees the light of day just as it is, with all its imperfections, it is because I have surrendered to friendly pleas assuring me that it would still be useful, despite the progress achieved in the last few years in France, especially as regards knowledge of British social anthropology.

For the principal purpose of these lectures was to introduce the French student to British anthropology, in a limited but concrete fashion, through the study of a single theory in the work of the authors selected. The theory concerned, that of descent groups, is, moreover, central to this school. By way of contrast, and in order to avoid confusion and to put into greater relief the character and spirit of the British theory, I added a summary of the structural theory of kinship (or what we designate as such on this side of the Channel), or more exactly of its restricted form, which can be called the theory of marriage alliance. Though relatively more familiar here, the latter nonetheless lacked a summary scientific form, and this was an opportunity to put one forward.

Before entering into this, and in order to connect the first and second theories, Part I presents and discusses the idea of kinship in general. The British school, and more particularly Radcliffe-Brown, provides our point of departure, but the analysis brings out the beginnings of the second theory as well.

I have mentioned avoiding confusion between the two theories. There was in the past, as there is in the present and threatens to be in the future, a tendency to exploit them simultaneously without realizing their profound heterogeneity. It was this danger above all which

---

[1] 'Enseignement préparatoire à la recherche approfondie en sciences sociales' (Preparatory teaching for advanced research in the social sciences), organised for a limited number of students by the Ecole Pratique des Hautes Etudes, 6th Section, and recognised by an official diploma.

appeared to me to necessitate a clear comparison at the level of principles as a pre-condition for any future progress (which by no means
rules out combining the two theories advisedly, should the need arise).
I considered this to be one of the solid foundations from which young
apprentice researchers could not only prepare new analyses in the
domain of kinship, but even adopt a reasonably certain view of the
totality of the domain of anthropology.

I have been less clear than I would have wished on a related point,
but it is one on which, unlike the preceding one, there is no need to be
categorical, no matter how convinced one might be. It will be noted
that I have been careful to take the theories concerned in their
restricted aspect, in which they have been or might be treated scientif-
ically, and not in their metaphysical aspect, as it were. In their
restricted aspect, each of these theories offers an account of the major
aspects of a *certain type of system*. This is a reasonable assumption to
make. Neither so far has acquired any scientific title to universality.
Such at least is my conviction. Rather, we shall need other restricted
theories for other types of system before we can anticipate a truly universal theory. Thus the systems called 'cognatic' by some, 'undifferentiated' by others, will only be elucidated by an ad hoc theory, and
contemporary efforts to achieve this, whether through an extension of
the concept of descent which deprives the latter of all content or by
recourse to the passage from 'elementary' structures to the supposed
'complex structures', are in my opinion condemned in advance. Apart
from the fact that the proof of this proposition will only be provided by
results, a critical discussion of the suggested extensions would have
made us pass from a presentation of what has been established to a
totally different sort of consideration.

The teaching of EPRASS, of which these lectures form a part, com-
prised intensive work by students consisting mainly of small blocks of
controlled reading. The present account aimed above all to provide
them with a solid grasp of certain fundamental ideas. This is why,
rather than a more or less arbitrary yet comprehensive resumé, I have
preferred as much as possible to provide a detailed analytical commentary on chosen texts, aiming at accuracy rather than elegance,
and not ruling out repetition. This procedure has the advantage of
opening the way to a critical interpretation which it was not thought
necessary to avoid. Actually, it is characteristic of the present state of
anthropology that consensus is very limited and that it progresses by
radical steps rather than by quiet accumulation. An introduction,
even an elementary one, which gave no idea of this state of affairs
would be incomplete, perhaps false. Here the lecturer, a researcher
rather than a teacher, has pursued fundamental reflection beyond the
point where agreement among specialists ceases: where necessary, he

has simply marked clearly the point where, unfortunately, development becomes individual through the introduction of 'personal' commentaries. Will he be condemned for going this far? He was attempting to reach a view of the totality, and the transmission he was asked to effect from one generation to another would otherwise have seemed devalued to him.

The basic works used in the text have been assembled in a brief bibliography, and their study beyond the isolated passages quoted is recommended. They are not many, and an inspection of this list, and of the table of contents, will give the reader an idea of the limits that have been set. The texts are indicated in the order of their appearance in the text; they are referred to where necessary by number.

It is impossible to conceal a certain degree of disparity in the fact that marriage alliance, in Part III, is not treated entirely in the same manner as what precedes it. Perhaps it may be granted that, though its treatment may be different, the spirit is the same.

Louis Dumont
July 1970

PREFACE TO THE TEL EDITION

I would like to thank Gallimard and the Tel series for reissuing a work that has long been out of print, even though it might seem rather specialized. I like to think that there is a similarity here to an earlier situation, when my first book, *La Tarasque*, which appeared in the series L'espèce humaine, edited by Michel Leiris, received the patronage of Jean Paulhan and Gallimard. The similarity is in the originality that the anthropological dimension confers on the present book, as with the earlier one. In both cases, the discursiveness to which the reader is accustomed is opposed or complicated by the promotion of detail practised by anthropology in the name of the meaning of wholes.

In the present case, what is involved is a sort of report on a very special teaching project that had enjoyed great success. This teaching was based on the controlled reading of certain selected texts by students divided into small groups, with the aim that apprentice researchers should obtain a solid grasp of fundamental ideas.

When the book appeared in 1971, like the teaching that had preceded it, it was a case of rigorous innovation in order to offer a reduced but solid basis for the training of both students and researchers. Starting from precise details, it was necessary to evoke the spirit of these two schools of thought, in both of which the author has had an opportunity to participate. Today, after an interval of 25 years, and given the changes in the ideological landscape of the social sciences that have intervened in the meantime, it is to be expected that the book may be read a little differently. The odds are that the contemporary reader will have his attention drawn above all by the contrast between the two styles of thought that flourished here in the genesis of a single social science. (Let us merely hope that the reader does not lose too much patience over the details, cautions and limitations that this approach involves.)

It is this global aspect, touching closely on the comparison of national cultures, that my much lamented colleague Maurice Freedman, a London sinologist who succeeded Evans-Pritchard in the chair of social anthropology at Oxford, chose to highlight in his review of the present work (*Man*, Vol. 7, no. 4, 1972, pp. 654–55).

L.D.

Professor A.R. Radcliffe-Brown
Reproduced with the permission of the Institute of Social and Cultural Anthropology.

Professor Meyer Fortes
Reproduced with the permission of the Institute of Social and Cultural Anthropology.

Professor E.E. Evans-Pritchard
Reproduced with the permission of the Institute of Social and Cultural Anthropology.

Professor Claude Lévi-Strauss
Reproduced with the permission of the Institute of Social and Cultural Anthropology.

Professor Louis Dumont
Reproduced with the permission of the Institute of Social and Cultural Anthropology.

PART I

KINSHIP IN THE WORK OF
RADCLIFFE-BROWN

A. WHAT IS KINSHIP?

1. *Notes and Queries*

The British have difficulties with their own language when it comes to defining kinship. Let us start with *Notes and Queries*, the general guide for the researcher published by the Royal Anthropological Institute in London (bibliog. no. 1). The 1951 edition turns to kinship after dealing with the family. The article 'Kinship' begins:

> The bonds of marriage, parenthood and siblingship ... which connect the members of the elementary family with one another result in a network of *relationships by kinship and affinity*. (p. 75, my emphasis)

It is difficult to translate this passage literally into French. The reference to the elementary family links it with what precedes. One recognises the three elementary relations of kinship: the marriage relationship, the relationship between parent(s) and children or relation of filiation, and the relationship between brothers and sisters, regardless of sex, or, as we would say, between *germains* (siblingship). 'Affinity' is understood as relationships which include an element of marriage. We see in the final words, those I have emphasised, that the British have no word to designate kinship in the sense of including relations of affinity or 'by alliance'. For 'relations of kinship' in general, they are obliged to say 'relations of kinship and affinity'. In French this would be rendered, more exactly than in the passage emphasised, as *relations de consanguinité et d'affinité* ['relationships of consanguinity and affinity', RP] (since consanguinity and affinity are mutually exclusive). A point to be kept in mind is that 'kinship', which can sometimes be translated by *parenté*, signifies more precisely consanguinité ['consanguinity', RP].

Personal Commentary

Here, therefore, British anthropology is handicapped by the English language in its lack of any indispensable general term. In this respect things are happier in French, but we shall encounter the reverse situation shortly. Here is a interesting problem for the establishment of a scientific terminology: the anthropologist needs scientific terms, but if he is not to lose all contact with social reality, he is obliged to choose his terms with respect to *their meaning in the language* in which he is writing. He may well tend to respect the usage given in authoritative dictionaries, but in a case like the present there is a conflict between this usage and scientific needs. What is to be done in such a situation? One suggestion is that it would be best to start by characterising the usage concerned and if possible understanding it, and then to remedy the conflict by moving away from the usage in the most suitable fashion. In the present case the usage is peculiar to English. As to its sense, its function does not consist at all, as one might expect, in giving any importance to affinity. Quite the contrary, this usage is related to the fact that in our societies affinity is devalued: affinal relationships are temporary, my brother-in-law is an uncle (a consanguineal relative) to my children. Whereas French still has special terms in certain cases (*bru* and *gendre*), English only has secondary determinants: 'son-in-law, daughter-in-law'. Comparatively – the point cannot be expanded here – the dichotomy in English usage corresponds to a sort of apotheosis of consanguinity and a concomitant devaluation of affinity. For general theory, particularly with regard to the societies we shall be considering in Part III, there is something exceptional here that a scientific terminology must transcend while giving it its due.

Most happily, we are in a position to do this in French without altering the sense or resorting to neologisms, since for us *parenté* includes kinship by affinity or, as we say, 'by alliance', as well as kinship in the restricted sense of consanguinity. (See Littré, Dictionnaire, under *Parent*: '4. By extension, allies: "He became my relative by marrying my cousin"'.)

Here might be raised a problem relating to French usage itself. I have translated 'kinship' as *consanguinité* [consanguinity, RP] by quite naturally opposing consanguinity and affinity. This usage is perfectly understandable: consanguines are then all relatives save affinal ones. One might object that, although this is the usage of canon law and elsewhere, it is different in modern civil law, where only paternal relatives are called consanguines. Should we therefore adopt for the term 'consanguine' its sense in French law, thus putting ourselves in contradiction with Anglo-Saxon anthropological usage (Morgan: *Systems of Consanguinity and Affinity*) and depriving ourselves of the sole clear and available term to designate relationships other than those of affinity, or should we adopt the way chosen here? Two observations can be made: (1) there is much less inconvenience in contradicting a special juridical usage than in contradicting familiar usage, in which alone we really live: social anthropology cannot commit itself to total compliance with the categories of the jurists, whose preoccupations are stricter than its own; (2) the way we have chosen is convenient at the global level (kinship = consanguinity plus affinity) and is international, and it creates a difficulty only at a level which is entirely secondary: this is a good reason to prefer it.

Notes and Queries continues:

> Kinship is a relationship actually or putatively traced through parent–child or sibling relations, and *recognized for social purposes.* (p. 75, my emphasis)

We see that: (1) once affinity is left aside, we are left with two other elementary relations of kinship; (2) stress is laid on the fact that consanguineal relationships are not necessarily 'real' or biological (in the case of adoption, for example) and that what counts as and what, properly speaking, characterises kinship is its social recognition; (3) in this passage, the word 'kinship' signifies at once 'consanguinity' in respect of the two relationships mentioned and 'kinship' in respect of the social character of the institution, which evidently includes relations of affinity.

We have here an example of the ambiguities to which English usage inevitably leads. This was felt by Radcliffe-Brown himself:

> I shall use the term 'kinship system' as short for a system of kinship and marriage. ... It is a pity that there is no inclusive term in English for all relationships which result from the existence of family and marriage. It would be very tiresome to speak all the time of a system of kinship and affinity. I hope, therefore, that my use of the term will be accepted. *It need not lead to ambiguity.* (*Structure and Function*, p. 51, bibliog. no. 2, my emphasis)

2. Radcliffe-Brown

In a passage in 'The Study of Kinship Systems' (1941, *Structure and Function*, pp. 51–52, bibliog. no. 2), Radcliffe-Brown gives a formula very close to the one cited earlier from *Notes and Queries*: 'The existence of the elementary family creates three special kinds of social relationship....' In his Introduction to *African Systems of Kinship and Marriage* (1950, bibliog. no. 3), he writes somewhat differently:

> Two persons are kin when one is descended from the other ... or when they are both descended from a common ancestor. [...] Kinship ... results from the *recognition of a social relationship* between parents and children ... (p. 4, my emphasis)

This passage recalls the last passage cited from *Notes and Queries* in the stress it places on the social nature of kinship (my emphasis, but see below, §7). It differs in that siblingship is left aside, consanguinity thus being linked only to the relation of filiation (elementary) or descent (multiple), a nuance to be noted in the way the French term *fil-iation* is used.[1] Implicitly, therefore, siblingship is reduced to filiation, and in effect the relationship between brothers and sisters can be seen as resulting from a double relation of filiation: (from brother or sister to their common parents. Let us note another nuance: filiation is the relationship with one or both parents). Starting from three elementary relations, we are now reduced to only one by the fact of language on the one hand and Radcliffe-Brown's decision on the other. His choice contains a paradox: if there are three elementary relations of kinship, including two elementary relations of consanguinity, and if, on the other hand, one insists that kinship is a social, not a biological matter, what benefit is there in reducing a simple relation of siblingship to a double relation of filiation? If it is a matter of reducing consanguinity to a single principle, it seems that this principle can only be biological (something like 'procreation'). It is not entirely this that is at issue for Radcliffe-Brown. We shall see later a probable reason for his preference in the particular importance that he, and British anthropology in general, give to descent and to the groups that are formed through it (see §10). Let us note also that the reduction of siblingship to descent or filiation is common in our own culture. In civil law as in canon law, one measures the 'degree' of kinship between two individuals by going back to their common ancestor. In this view, affinity is relatively devalued, and kinship tends to become merged with descent. In other words, descent becomes in some way the essence of kinship and the other relations become attributes of this essence. One can appreciate the success of this way of seeing things, one which, moreover, tends to bring to the fore the 'biological' aspect of things. Unfortunately, it is not a comparative point of view, and whenever it claims to be, sociocentrism is introduced.

We shall retain for our own use two things out of all this: that kinship is a social or conventional matter, whatever its links with human reproduction (we shall return to this, §7); and that it appears in three elementary forms: marriage or affinity, siblingship, and descent or filiation. But in saying this, we are doing no more than making a little more precise what we knew already. When we ask, 'What is kinship?', we are thinking of something like a particular type of social phenomenon or a domain of social life about which we would like to know, for the purposes of our study, its beginning and its end, the nature of its relationship with the rest of social life, its principal aspects, articulations and components, how to regard it, and how to compare it from one society to another.

---

[1] [In other words, French *filiation* is used to translate both 'filiation' (ties between parents and children) and 'descent' (the extension of such ties backwards in time from the perspective of the present) from English, RP.]

B. THE MEANING OF 'KINSHIP SYSTEM'

3. The Principle

In designating this domain or aspect of social organisation, in English we encounter the expression 'kinship system', with the warning, as already explained, that this is an abstraction for 'system of kinship and affinity'. Thus *Notes and Queries*:

> It is convenient to use the term *kinship system* (short for system of kinship and affinity) to denote the pattern of social usages observed in the reciprocal behaviour of persons who are, or who are regarded as being, related by kinship and affinity. (ibid.: 76, original emphasis)

It will be noted here – apart from the earlier remark and the renewed emphasis on the conventional aspect of kinship – that the kinship system designates a 'pattern of social usages observed in the reciprocal behaviour of related persons'. Or, again, the kinship system is the set of regularities that can be abstracted from the *behaviour* towards one another of individuals in a relation of kinship. In other words, kinship constitutes a system because behaviour in various relations of kinship forms a system or presupposes an underlying system which it is the task of the anthropologist to formalise. This interpretation strains the English text a little, but is more or less implied by it.

Radcliffe-Brown expresses himself somewhat differently to begin with:

> A system of kinship and marriage can be looked at as an arrangement which enables persons to live together and co-operate with one another in an orderly social life. ('Introduction', p. 3)

Here, the word 'system' translates the idea of an ordered arrangement, or more precisely something which (1) functions effectively; (2) corresponds more or less to an order. Let us note also that there is nothing in this definition differentiating social life in general from kinship in particular. This is explicable, in the sense that in tribal ('primitive, archaic' or, relatively speaking, simple) societies, the whole or the greater part of social life is expressed in the language of kinship. However (*Structure and Function*, p. 53), the network of kinship relations is only one part of social structure. Let us consider some of Radcliffe-Brown's other formulations. In the same text, he stresses that the facts of kinship constitute a system or 'whole'. It is necessary, he says, to compare and analyse, but analysis can 'only be applied to something that is itself a whole or synthesis'. By analysis, 'we separate out the components of a complex whole and thereby discover the relation of these components to one another within the whole' ('Introduction', p. 2). But, we might ask, what is a whole, and how do we know when we are dealing with one?

The author poses the question most clearly in his article 'The Study of Kinship Systems':

> ... by using the word 'system' I have made an assumption, an important and far-reaching assumption, for that word implies that whatever it is applied to is a complex unity, an organised whole. My explicit hypothesis is that between the various features of a particular kinship system there is a complex relation of interdependence. The formulation of this working hypothesis leads immediately to the method of sociological analysis, by which we seek to discover the nature of kinship systems as systems, if they be really such. For this purpose we need to make a systematic comparison of a sufficient number of sufficiently diverse systems. We must compare them, not in reference to single, superficial, and therefore immediately observable characters, but as wholes, as systems, and in reference, therefore, to general characters which are only discovered in the process of comparison. Our purpose is to arrive at valid abstractions or general ideas in terms of which the phenomena can be described and classified. (Structure and Function, pp. 53–54)

I have quoted this important passage in its entirety, though it hardly resolves the problems of how one characterises the 'organised whole' in question, of how one defines the traits of the kinship system, or of where its boundary with other social facts is located. It seems that the system ends where the awareness of kinship ties ends (ibid., middle of p. 53).

4. Characteristics of 'Kinship Systems' according to Radcliffe-Brown

Radcliffe-Brown clarifies the contents of the kinship system for us, coming near to *Notes and Queries* when he writes:

> ... a kinship system ... is in the first place a system of dyadic relations between person and person in a community, the behaviour of any two persons [finding themselves, LD] in any of these relations being regulated in some way, and to a greater or less extent, by social usage. (ibid., pp. 52–53)

The words 'in the first place' are to be noted here. There are other things in a kinship system than simply interpersonal relationships. Briefly, there are also the names people use to designate or to address their relatives, the ideas they have concerning kinship, defined social groups (including the 'domestic family'), relations with the dead ('ancestor worship') (ibid., p. 53) and finally group relationships which correspond to descent groups ('Introduction', p. 84; see also below, §6). But, in respect of all this, interpersonal relationships occupy a central position and constitute 'the reality of a kinship system as part of a social structure' (ibid., p. 10). We shall return to this. First let us follow Radcliffe-Brown up to what is perhaps the final statement of his theoretical thinking on this point. Kinship systems are based on 'structural principles', about which, towards the end of the 'Introduction', the following is said:

> Just as an architect in designing a building has to make a choice of structural principles which he will use, so, though in less deliberate fashion, in the construction of a kinship system there are a certain number of structural principles which can be used and combined in various ways. It is on the selection, method of use, and combination of these principles that the character of the structure depends. A structural analysis of a kinship system must therefore be in terms of structural principles and their application. ('Introduction', p. 83)

We notice already here that this concerns not universal principles that would apply everywhere, but the different 'structural' characteristics of different types of system, which are conceived of as variously making use of certain elements or combinations of elements. I shall go into details in due course (§§9-10).

5. Sketch of a Theory of 'Systems'

Let us reflect on what we have just been reading. We have encountered the question of what is a 'whole'. For us, what differentiates a 'whole' from a simple collection, independently of any idea of organism or of functioning, is its being ordered internally in a discernible fashion. Ultimately and logically, in contrast to a collection, a 'whole' is an ensemble founded on distinctive oppositions which determine a complementarity between its elements. A single opposition will suffice: a man is a whole, in the traditional view, in so far as he is 'composed' of a body and a soul.

We have seen *Notes and Queries* refer to a certain arrangement or pattern of relations which forms them into a whole. From this point of view, British anthropology, in so far as it tends to reduce kinship to a single essence, seems to diverge from the construction of kinship as a true 'whole'. It would be better to return to the idea implicit in the title of Morgan's *Systems of Consanguinity and Affinity of the Human Family*. For certain societies, at least (see Part 3), the opposition of consanguinity and affinity really does constitute kinship as a whole. Evans-Pritchard, coming after Radcliffe-Brown, is very explicit here:

> Kinship categories are limited in number and they have a definite arrangement to any person. It is not merely that the anthropologist perceives that they have a pattern. The Nuer himself perceives it and can describe it without reference to any particular person... as an abstract system. [...] ... there is a recognized balance between the kin on the father's side and the kin on the mother's side ... (*Kinship and Marriage*, p. 152, bibliog. no. 9)

We already have here – and shall come across it again in a more exact form in the same author – a structural notion of the interdependence of kinship 'traits' of which Radcliffe-Brown spoke.

Personal Commentary

To try to be a little more precise, let us invoke the theory of wholes. Let there be a whole A and an element a of that whole. The proposition that must always be kept in mind in sociology is that a (in itself) is different from 'a as part of the whole A': $|a|^A$. We are used to saying that such and such a trait is the same in one type of society and in another, but that its place or function in or relation to the whole differs. Strictly speaking, this is a defective form of expression: although we are considering wholes or 'systems', a trait *which does not have the same place is not the same*. For example, we speak of a 'preference for marriage with the cross cousin' in a society with exogamous groups which distinguishes rigorously between parallel and cross relatives; if we speak similarly of a 'preference for marriage' with the patrilateral [for *patrilinéaire* in the original, RP] parallel cousin in an Islamic or Arab society where there are no exogamous groups and where the arrangement of categories is totally different, we lose sight of the system, and we speak as if it were the simple and isolated trait of 'marriage preference' (normative or statistical) which interested us. But this 'preference' is not the same thing, sociologically speaking, in the two systems. Similarly again, let us suppose another whole ('system') A', of which a can be taken to form a part:

$$|a|^A \text{ is different from } |a|^{A'}.$$

For this reason, it is very important for us to be able to trace the boundary of the 'system' we are claiming to isolate.

In the foregoing, the word 'system' refers to interdependence *within* a certain boundary. But this is not all, for the same word also refers to what goes on *outside* it. In effect, whenever we speak of a 'kinship system', we are asserting in brief that it is legitimate to isolate such a system from the total society in such a way that the elements within the system will be taken as interdependent with one another, but not with those outside it. If Σ is the total social system, we assume in brief that the elements of Σ can be attached, according to circumstance, to the kinship sub-system S1, to the other sub-systems S2, S3, etc., in such a way that the global interdependence can be reduced through simplification to two sorts of interdependence: that of the elements (like a) within a sub-system, and that of the *sub-systems with one another*. Moreover, and under the same conditions, we think we can compare the kinship sub-systems S1 and S'1 of the different societies Σ and Σ' while disregarding Σ and Σ'.

Radcliffe-Brown speaks incidentally of the relationship between kinship systems and 'other parts of the social system' – religion, political organisation, economic life ('Introduction', towards foot of p. 84). The distribution of social reality into different sub-systems is very clear in Evans-Pritchard:

> We have dealt in this book mainly with the family, the kinship system, and the lineage system, and we have discussed their relations to one another [these three systems or aspects, LD] in the whole society, particularly in terms of its political structure [fourth system, LD] [...] the values of the different social systems operate in different situations and at different levels of social life. (*Kinship and Marriage*, p. 180, bibliog. no. 9)

The 'systems' here correspond to what we have above called sub-systems. Let us note that 'kinship system' has a more restricted meaning here than for Radcliffe-Brown, since not only is the lineage system distinguished from it, but even relationships within the family (see §6).

There is one observation to be made concerning the nature of the sub-systems which it is hoped to distinguish within the global social system. To begin with there will doubtless be a tendency to see an empirical separation here, as if what were involved were sifting in social reality whatever comes under kinship, religion or the economy, classifying all this separately, and then reconstituting the image of the totality by juxtaposing these fragments as in a puzzle. Such a viewpoint is convenient for a preliminary classification or rapid description. But the interest of a systematic examination is that it makes us penetrate further: it becomes no longer a matter of distinguishing facts, but of distinguishing the point of view of an analyst proceeding more or less in line with indigenous ideas. It is very clear, for example, that a given fact will often have *at the same time* an aspect of kinship, an aspect of religion, etc. In other words, the ideal sub-systems are partly retrieved when seen from the point of view of observed facts. There is no inconvenience involved here, since the aim is to analyse and express more easily the coherence of the global social reality.

Personal Commentary

In short, what one is led to, still speaking ideally, is the application to global social reality of partial points of view, each of which may have the property of separating out a 'whole' in the sense of a totality or a system structured by its internal oppositions. Supposing the analysis to be complete, the global society will be seen as a system of relations of two orders: relations between sub-systems or partial wholes, and relations within each of the partial wholes. We shall see immediately that things are not so simple in the case of kinship, however privileged it may be.

In reflecting on this, we have moved away from the practice that is most current among contemporary specialists. Certainly this practice makes frequent use of (special sub-) systems, but their definition is less rigorous than that proposed above. It is the exigencies of comparison that are responsible for this divergence, whether they are real or only apparent. It must certainly be stressed that the way proposed in our text *does not guarantee the possibility of comparison at the level of the sub-systems*. In reality, the definition of a given sub-system depends on the society it relates to, and another society may very well not accept such a definition. To take a very simple example: Evans-Pritchard isolated a sub-system of descent groups among the Nuer, but societies that lack descent groups obviously will not recognise such a sub-system. The comparison is only guaranteed at the level of the global society, and on the whole it is in perfect accord with his procedure of monographic analysis that Evans-Pritchard was later able to declare that no typology or comparison was possible at the level of the parts, that anthropology can only juxtapose descriptions (of societies or) of different types of society, and that it is not a science but rather a sort of historiography (*Essays in Social Anthropology*, pp. 13-28). If, on the other hand, one wishes to maintain the comparison at the level of the parts and compare not only political or economic systems, but even something like 'systems of social stratification', the idea of these systems will not be provided by the coherence of the corresponding domain (or of the object from the corresponding point of view) in a given society, but by the comparative requirement itself, the anthropologist assuming that in every society there must exist data pertaining to the partial approach he has chosen and which will form a system only in the sense that they satisfy his preoccupation with neatly partitioned comparison. Although this attitude is based on an a priori classification of social phenomena, is in no way preoccupied with reconstituting the whole of a society and more or less sacrifices the indigenous ideology, it makes partial comparison easy. The other attitude, which is certainly less widespread, being based on the global society and its indigenous representations, is able to go beyond its own viewpoint, but it is true that it complicates comparison by articulating it no longer on classes of phenomena but on *types* of society.

1970 Addition

The preceding is very inadequate in several respects. Above all, the distinctive opposition is not the only one that ought to be considered: this is so only if one abstracts the hierarchy, as we tend to do in our modern culture. It is necessary to add to it hierarchical opposition, essentially the relationship of an element to the whole of which it is a part and which, although less simple than distinctive opposition, is no less to be taken as an immediate datum, elementary and irreducible. Now it is evident that every time we speak of a whole which 'functions', an 'organism', an ensemble oriented towards an 'end' or the 'function' of an element in an ensemble, we are implicitly assuming such a subordination of the element to the ensemble. We even get an inkling here that the aversion of the moderns towards hierarchy is linked to their aversion towards teleology and is responsible for the failure of 'functionalism'. However, we sometimes see hierarchy reappear, sometimes distinctly, at the level of concrete scientific works, whether in biology or even sociology or psychology. (More profoundly, a hierarchical premise is fundamentally hidden beneath the individualist atomism which dominates the modern world and which says: 'ultimate ends merge with those of each human individual taken in isolation', adding: 'his liberty is limited only by those of his fellows', but omitting: 'his liberty subordinates everything else', i.e. 'this liberty is established upon the subordination of all the ends which are not those of the individual and which thus cease to be the ultimate ones'.)

In the second place, whenever our colleagues speak, as it seems frequently these days, of a 'political system', a 'system of social stratification', etc., this seems to contain two presuppositions: a) that a society constitutes a whole whose elements are directly linked and interdependent, b) that one can adopt the particular view of this interdependence that the viewpoint of our society suggests (political'), more or less refined where necessary by sociological considerations (as in the expression 'social stratification'). The two things go together, for if we were to criticise one of these viewpoints – that of stratification, for example – as arbitrary and perhaps illegitimate, others might reply: 'If social facts are so highly and strictly interdependent, what does the point of view applied to them matter, since there will always remain enough interdependence in the end?' Here certainly is an illusion whose fallaciousness we point out. Such a notion is always implicit in the use of the word 'system' concerning every selection made more or less arbitrarily in the data: although the particular 'system' may be only very slightly systematic, it is in fact guaranteed by the global system. From the supposedly inaccessible 'whole', we extract for convenience aspects that are not wholes, what might be called 'nominal systems' as opposed to 'real systems', which are real for the subjects themselves, real in spirit.

A third observation consists in relating the two preceding ones: in ordinary or let us say inferior accounts of 'systems', i.e. of nominal systems, there is at once an affirmation and a denial of hierarchy. The affirmation is contained in the proposition that what is found among ourselves must be found elsewhere: in other words, modern society suffices to provide the co-ordinates of reference, i.e. it is implicitly conceived as superior to the others (despite the denials of authors, however much made in good faith), this being what I have called sociocentrism. The denial of hierarchy is multiple, present at all levels, ubiquitous. It necessarily results, moreover, from the choice of egalitarian society as the privileged reference point.

In short, and so as not to be unfair towards the consideration of nominal systems, i.e. those which are not those of the subjects themselves, it is necessary to say that at best this is founded *at one and the same time* on the notion of the coherence of the social data, whatever they may be – a notion which is in reality exaggerated and almost mystical – and on the notion of the supremacy of modern society.

6. The Different Aspects of Kinship

In theory, therefore, and in light of the preceding, a kinship system implies an intellectual construction, something like a 'model', in which all the parts or traits can be understood in relation to the whole, while neglecting everything left outside the system. In reality, we have already seen, and shall see more precisely here, that the domain of kinship includes diverse aspects which hardly make a system when taken together and besides are studied most unevenly by different authorities. The domain has split up, as it were, under the impact of different points of view, only some of which correspond to systems in the strict sense. This splitting, this differentiation, is clearly seen if one goes back to Marcel Mauss. In British anthropology, Radcliffe-Brown decisively severed cultural history from sociological study, which were still mixed in the teaching of Mauss. Likewise, in the domain we are concerned with, Mauss spoke of what he called 'politico-domestic organs' (*Manuel d'ethnographie*, p. 124). Now in British practice this single heading is broken up into at least four different headings. Let us leave the 'political system' on one side. In isolating it (permanently in Britain, at any rate), Evans-Pritchard detached the lineage system or 'descent groups' from kinship – this is the first aspect. (Let us note straight away the new sense assumed by the word *filiation* in our translation, i.e. *filiation unilinéaire* [unilineal descent, RP]; see §11). Here we are definitely concerned with a system in the strict sense, and this distinction is accepted. Nevertheless, is it necessary to follow Evans-Pritchard and distinguish it absolutely from kinship? Radcliffe-Brown rejects this, perhaps through an attachment to the past:

> Professor Evans-Pritchard draws attention to the difference between the dyadic, person to person, relationships *that every kinship system includes*, and the group relationships that are established by a system of lineages or clans. They are, of course, both included in what has been called here a kinship system ... ('Introduction', p. 84, my emphasis)

The words emphasised contain an argument: if kinship systems in the global sense of the term are compared, it is obviously necessary to include within them the sub-system of groups, wherever it exists. Moreover, kin categories in the abstract sense underlie the system of descent groups. Finally, the development of British anthropology since Evans-Pritchard justifies the viewpoint of Radcliffe-Brown; moreover, the comparison between two schools of thought, which is our goal here, demands it.

We can then follow Radcliffe-Brown and say that the central part of the kinship system is constituted by interpersonal relations. This is the second aspect, though here are united on the one hand the kin categories or terms, and on the other attitudes in the widest sense (including the 'important occasions' or ceremonies emphasised by Evans-Pritchard, and not only day-to-day behaviour). (We shall come back to the relationship between categories and attitudes in §8.) Finally, one must attach to kinship both groups like the family (and the household or hearth) and institutions like marriage (consisting on the one hand of the complex of ceremonies and prestations, and on the other of the more or less jural condition). This is the third aspect, which in itself hardly forms a system in the strict sense, given, for example, the preponderance of the economic aspect in the family. We have cited above a passage in which Evans-Pritchard rigorously distinguishes between the family on the one hand and the kinship system, i.e. relations between kin, on the other. For this author, 'kin relations' exclude intra-familial relationships. He gives two reasons for this: the family is a group while kinship is not. One would then expect intra-familial relationships to be included as such among kin relations. To this, the author counters that the two kinds of relationship are 'certainly not for a Nuer' of the same order (*Kinship and Marriage*, p. 152). To the extent that the fact is not general, we have here an example of the obstacles that the rigour of a monographic study can place in the way of comparison.

Finally, there is a fourth aspect. We can assume that the various abstract traits by which we are accustomed to characterise a kinship system make a system: rules of filiation, residence, inheritance, succession, marriage rules, etc. must entail certain necessary relationships. We shall see that Radcliffe-Brown touches on this question in respect of his 'structural principles'. But he soon turns away from it, and it is only with Lévi-Strauss that we shall again encounter it systematically (below, Part 3).

7. The Nature of Kinship: A Recent Discussion

Having acquired some idea of what is involved in the study of kinship, we can now turn to a very recent discussion of its nature (bibliog. no. 4). In several publications, Ernest Gellner has called into question what has become the credo of the anthropologist in this matter, the essentially social nature of kinship relationships, and to insist on the biological aspect in so far as it is inescapably contained in them and must therefore ultimately be the key to them. The decisive answer to this trend has long been that the biological aspect is universal and cannot be the basis of observed differences, which are, let us remember, considerable, according to the type of society or, if one prefers, culture, and which emerge immediately as conventional, 'arbitrary', in a word social – as relevant to culture, not to nature, as Lévi-Strauss would say. Naturally Gellner can always stress that all societies ground kinship to some extent on a biological given, but, to continue following Lévi-Strauss here, what makes them societies is the way in which they move away from this given, interpreting it and modifying it, and not the biological residue which remains in all their constructions.

On this point, Beattie – concerned, it would seem, to establish an insuperable distance between the two aspects – has asserted that kinship is pure language or pure form, and that the content of this language, far from being biological, is of a totally different order: political, economic, etc. Schneider has criticised Beattie's view, arguing – with reason, it would seem – that kinship is not only language, that it is, like everything at this level, as much content as language. Schneider concludes by bringing together the 'kinship system' and the other systems that anthropology distinguishes. Here, where, for example, the 'political system' is concerned, a distinction will be called for: the language of kinship is, in general – concerning tribal societies, at any rate – an *indigenous* language; when we have made a complete inventory of all the kinship terms with all their meanings, etc., we have a sort of indigenous sketch of the external limits of the system, and *for that reason* we can hope to discover the law of interdependence which prevails within it. The language of politics, on the contrary – at any rate, for a great number of societies – is a *language imported by the observer*, and there is no guarantee that the 'system' defined according to this language is actually valid for a given society or that the same degree of interdependence can be established as could be expected in the earlier case. A system is really a kinship system to the extent that it corresponds effectively to the thought and language of the subjects themselves. This debate is highly instructive in so far as it leads to an impasse in wishing to acknowledge a pre-eminent status (content) in the categories of the society to which the anthropologist belongs in relation to that which he is studying (form).

Personal Commentary

See the preceding commentary. We define what is really involved in the dualism postulated in Beattie's formula if we remark that to begin with social facts become facts, or are known to us, always and only *through and thanks to ideas* (a language), and then that they are known to us in two different ways according to whether we have recourse to the ideas of the subjects themselves or to our own. Beattie's suggestion, in which he distinguishes form and content, 'language' and substantial reality, is actually a comparative proposition. From the indigenous point of view, there is a language which sufficiently expresses social reality. From the point of view of the anthropologist reporting implicitly or explicitly what he observes through his own experience in his own society, there is something in observed reality other than what those concerned see in it themselves. The opposition is not between form and content, but between what is known directly in the categories of the society studied and what is known *indirectly* through the mediation of the categories of the anthropologist's own society. Are we to speak here of supposedly objective categories of sociology? My response is that, in the present situation, they are only a form of the latter and can only be something else in so far as they become progressively transformed through comparison with societies that are very different from those of the observer. In this sense, social anthropology is – contrary to what there is sometimes a tendency to think – more advanced than sociology in the strict sense.

C. INTERPERSONAL RELATIONS AND 'STRUCTURAL PRINCIPLES'

8. Interpersonal Relations: Terminology and Behaviour

We have noted that, in his 'Introduction', Radcliffe-Brown recommended the study of the kinship terminology, i.e. the totality of terms which are used to call and designate relatives (respectively terms of address and terms of reference), but he declared also that behaviour, or attitudes, represent the heart, the 'reality', of the kinship system. Furthermore:

> In the actual study of a kinship system the nomenclature is of the utmost importance. It affords the best possible approach to the investigation and analysis of the kinship system as a whole. This, of course, it could not do if there were no real relations of interdependence between the terminology and the rest of the system. (*Structure and Function*, p. 62)

These relations are 'relations within an ordered whole' (p. 61), and the author maintains, in opposition to Kroeber, that 'all over the world there are important correspondences between kinship nomenclature and social practices' (ibid.). These statements are important in themselves, but to understand their value and orientation fully it is necessary to place them in their historical context. The whole of the first part of 'The Study of Kinship Systems', from which the preceding quotations come, takes the form of a discussion directed against Rivers and Kroeber simultaneously. Radcliffe-Brown notes that originally anthropologists were interested in kinship terminologies because they considered them to be a historical precipitate of usages which have disappeared. For Morgan, 'systems of consanguinity and affinity' were in practice reducible to systems of kin terms, and he had recourse to the most unlikely historical hypotheses to explain the form these systems took. Moreover, Rivers explained the assimilation of different relations of kinship to the level of the terminology through supposed forms of marriage which have disappeared. Radcliffe-Brown condemns this recourse to 'conjectural history'. We may add that Malinowski contributed not a little to turning British anthropologists away from the analysis of terminologies in mocking this 'kinship algebra' (see, for example, Meyer Fortes in *American Anthropologist*, Vol. LV, 1953, p. 20, bibliog. no. 10). For Radcliffe-Brown, these diachronic speculations are to be replaced by a synchronic consideration of the relationship between kinship terms and kinship attitudes. He allies himself with Starcke, quoting a remarkable statement of his from 1889, according to which the terminology is 'the faithful reflection of the juridical relations which arise between the nearest kinsfolk' [quoted in *Structure and Function*, p. 59, RP]. We would be wrong in thinking that Radcliffe-Brown himself is assuming anything more here than the confirmation of a direct link between the two aspects (see his specific statement, p. 62 and note; also Lévi-Strauss, *Anthropologie structurale*, p. 46; see also the present text, §10). Later, he writes:

> As a general rule ... towards all persons to whom a given term of relationship is applied there is some element of attitude or behaviour by which the relationship is given recognition, even if it is only some feature of etiquette or an obligation to exhibit friendliness or respect. ('Introduction', p. 25)

The question posed at this point is to know whether, for the purposes of study, one must take terminology and attitudes together or separately. In fact, these two sub-totalities are presented empirically under different forms and, as we shall see later, they are far from corresponding exactly in detail. We are therefore led to consider them separately, and, up to a point, this is what Radcliffe-Brown does.

Radcliffe-Brown was well aware that attitudes make a system and that a particular relationship or type of attitude must be studied, and can only be understood, in relation to the system in its totality: so it is with the privileges of the uterine nephew in 'The Mother's Brother in South Africa' (1924), and joking relationships in a double article of 1940-1949 (both reproduced in *Structure and Function*; see the rather systematised resumé of the second theme by Meyer Fortes in the *British Journal of Sociology*, 1955, pp. 24–25). Unfortunately these developments are often confused because Radcliffe-Brown has a tendency to merge interpersonal attitudes into groups – on the one hand the family, about which we are going to say something in a minute, and on the other, and above all, the lineage. Thus it will be necessary to return to this matter after examining unilineal descent.

We have already noted a difficulty in the definition of the system of attitudes, which is linked to the fact that they become less and less intense the more remote the relationship, and that they melt away imperceptibly in the absence of kinship. 'Rules of behaviour are more definite and more important for near relatives than for more distant ones' ('Introduction', p. 25). Whence the tendency, which we can trace among other authors but is already noticeable here, to isolate for a given subject a circle of close relatives in which all attitudes will be presented with the maximum clarity, while more remote relationships will only reflect them in an increasingly indistinct fashion – a tendency, in short, to construct a microcosm or reduced model of kinship in the total sense with regard to attitudes. For Radcliffe-Brown, the elementary family plays this role to some extent: 'The unit of structure from which a kinship system is built up is the ... "elementary family"' (*Structure and Function*, p. 51). Here we might merely see a way of reducing interpersonal relations to 'groups', but this is no more than a part of what the author has in mind. In fact, he continues:

> The existence of the elementary family creates three special kinds of social relationships ...
>
> The three relationships that exist within the elementary family constitute what I call [relationships of, LD] the first order. Relationships of the second order are those which depend on the connection of two elementary families through a common member, and are such as father's father, mother's brother, wife's sister, and so on. In the third order are such as father's brother's son and mother's brother's wife. (ibid., pp. 51, 52)

What is interesting for us here is not so much the composition of elementary relationships in relations of the second and third orders, but rather the notion that the essence of relationships – and of attitudes – is found to be concentrated in some way in a small circle of relatives, identified here with the family. Thus as regards the privileges of the uterine nephew, the relationship between a nephew and his maternal uncle (and his other relatives on the maternal side) is 'derived' from that between the child and his mother in what is a patrilineal milieu (ibid., p. 29, nos. 4–5). In other passages, the same author seems inclined to see the element of kinship as the sibling group or the group of siblings and their mother ('Introduction', pp. 83–84).

We have already noted a clear idea of the structural character of the totality of kinship relationships in the work of Evans-Pritchard. A further passage by this same author leaves nothing to be desired in this respect:

> The balance between father's kin and mother's kin is always maintained on important occasions of social life, such as marriages, settlements of feuds, and religious feasts, when relationships are formally defined.

The balance is felt also by Nuer in their everyday life, and it strongly affects the relationships. A mother's brother, for example, is not just a mother's brother. He is, so to speak, a mother's brother and not a father's brother, and the fact that a man has a mother's brother towards whom he can turn in trouble affects his relations with his paternal kin. Relationships are tinged with their opposites. (*Kinship and Marriage*, p. 166, bibliog. no. 9)

The stress placed on ceremonies as 'important occasions' of social life is to be noted in this passage. This is not always evident when one speaks of 'behaviour' or 'attitudes', and it happens that this ceremonial aspect is relatively neglected in contemporary anthropology. But this quotation from Evans-Pritchard shows above all the sort of logic that is necessary in this study: not a logic of substance, but a structural logic, for which each relationship is what it is by virtue of its place in a whole. Let us add that this frame of mind is far from having dominated British anthropology since Evans-Pritchard, any more than, 'before' him, it did with Radcliffe-Brown.

Evans-Pritchard is scarcely interested in the kinship terminology at all, which is all the more striking in that in general he closely follows the conceptions of the Nuer as recorded in their language. No analysis of the system of kin terms is to be found in his books and, no doubt for this reason, not even a list of the terms themselves. As for attitudes, we have seen that he treats the family separately from extra-familial relationships. As for the latter, he isolates the circle of close relatives, of which other relatives constitute a sort of extension. In this circle are found what he calls the 'nuclear kin', the core of kinship (or of consanguinity) if one will, containing all the structural traits of the system of attitudes in general.

As this kinship core is structured and has nothing to do with the family, it naturally leads us to what Lévi-Strauss has called 'the atom of kinship' or the 'elementary structure of kinship', characterised as the smallest unit which contains the three elementary relations of kinship, without exclusive reference to the biological or reproductive aspects, but on the contrary with reference to the prohibition of incest as a universal social phenomenon, in so far as it involves the opposition between the brother–sister relationship and the husband–wife relationship. This is a matter of the unity formed by a man, his sister, her husband, and the child of the latter pair ('L'Analyse structurale...', in *Anthropologie structurale*, bibliog. no. 5).

We therefore find in all three of our authors a common tendency to isolate a core of kinship in which attitudes appear clearly through being contrasted.

At the same place, Lévi-Strauss makes clear the relationship between the 'terminological system' and the 'system of attitudes'.

Although there is no 'rigorous parallelism' between attitudes and terminology, the two orders are not autonomous:

> ... this relation of interdependence does not imply a one-to-one correlation. The system of attitudes constitutes, rather, a dynamic integration of the system of terminology. (47/38–39)

This is his final word, and it is not very explicit. The reason for this is perhaps that in the original article of 1945 from which these lines are taken, Lévi-Strauss brings into doubt, by reasoning, the possibility of a structural analysis of the kinship terminology, while he constructs for the analysis of attitudes the 'elementary structures' just mentioned. (The word 'system' therefore has only a very general sense in the quotation above.) Conversely, in his great book entitled (but in a completely different sense) *Les structures élémentaires de la parenté* (bibliog.. no. 14), the same author is much more attached to the terminologies than to behaviour in general (with the exception of the regulation of marriage). Since we shall return to this in Part 3 (§28), let us conclude for the present that none of the three authors we have considered proposes to treat the kinship terminology as a sub-system in the strict sense, i.e. as susceptible to independent analysis. The rejection in principle of such an analysis is clearly at the root of Radcliffe-Brown's critique of my own attempt to provide one (see *Man* 1953, no. 169).

9. Radcliffe-Brown's 'Structural Principles'

We have seen Radcliffe-Brown announcing a consideration of the 'structural principles' of kinship systems. We must note straight away that with Radcliffe-Brown we shall find hardly anything in this phrase that might strike us as structural, by which I mean the complementarities that he was aware of, for example, on the level of attitudes, as already emphasised. We have already seen these 'principles' presented as potentially present or absent in any given system. It is the same with those he believes he sees prevailing in the arrangement of the kinship terminologies, and which are valid, *mutatis mutandis*, for attitudes: (1) the principle of the unity of the sibling group: a tie of 'solidarity' unites brothers and sisters into one social group, this group being seen as a 'unity' by an outsider (*Structure and Function*, pp. 64ff.); (2) the principle of the distinction of generations (this being more strictly marked in the terminology); (3) the principle of the unity of the lineage as a group ('the lineage group'; as with 1, there is internal solidarity and unity when seen from the outside). At the level of the terminology, these principles are made to intervene whenever siblings or members of the same lineage are classed together in the same category, whenever homologous relatives of different generations are placed in different categories, etc. It is obvious that Radcliffe-Brown believes he has found, for 1 and 3, a correspondence between the system of attitudes and the system of vocabulary. But these 'principles' are not universal: siblings or members of the same lineage may or may not be classed together (sometimes within the same terminology). They may even contradict one another: whenever the members of the lineage are classed together, principle 2, the distinction of generations, is denied, and vice versa. Thus the 'principles' only designate tendencies which are differently combined in each case: they represent only an attempt to distinguish certain terminological traits from certain elementary 'attitudes' (one distinction, two solidarities).

Personal Commentary

In order to assess the value of the 'principle of the unity of the lineage group' in respect of the kinship terminology, the following little exercise may be carried out. Let us take as an example the Fox kinship terminology as Radcliffe-Brown treats it in Figs. 5 to 9 of his article (ibid., pp. 71–74), collecting it all together in a single figure by making as many of the various uses of the same term as possible coincide or converge, for example, 'grandfather' (considering only, for simplification, the male relatives of the generations preceding and equivalent to that of ego, for example). It will readily be seen that Radcliffe-Brown's 'principle' only explains the facts very incompletely. In particular, the assimilation of (generally three) men of different generations comes about either within the same lineage or between relatives of different lineages who have *married into the same lineage*, this second type of assimilation representing the reciprocal usage to the first. It is not a matter of (elements of) lineages *in themselves*, but, if one will, of lineages *seen through* intermarriage, or more exactly, of intermarriage in so far as it reunites lineal segments (three generations from the generation that gave the wife). Thus one calls 'father' men of other lineages who have married into the lineage of the mother. (This is not all, but it was only meant to be a limited exercise.)

There are a few indications in the same text of the relationship between the general, abstract traits which characterise a given kinship system. For example, the complementarity between form of marriage and mode of descent (and of consanguinity) is clearly marked: 'The contrast between father-right and mother-right is one between two types of marriage' ('Introduction', p. 77). And Radcliffe-Brown explains that in mother-right, from the point of view of jural relations, the sibling group is stressed at the expense of the marriage relationship, etc.

These are no more than isolated indications in the 'Introduction', and Radcliffe-Brown soon adopts a different posture. He speaks emphatically of the lineage as the 'major structural principle' of certain systems (p. 81) and indicates briefly what he calls the 'more important structural principles' (p. 13). In fact, there is only one, namely descent under its various forms.

10. The Main Principle: Descent

This fundamental passage must be reproduced in its entirety (I have emphasised three words for the sake of clarity):

> Two persons who are *kin* are related in one or other of two ways: either one is descended from the other, or they are both descended from a common ancestor. It is to be remembered that 'descent' here refers to the social relationship of parents and children, not to the physical relation. *Kinship* is thus based on *descent*, and what first determines the character of a kinship system is the way in which descent is recognized and reckoned.
> ('Introduction', p. 13)

Let us note the words 'kinship [or consanguinity, LD] is based on descent'. This is a very arbitrary view in the form in which it is presented. Let us continue. Four modes of descent can be distinguished, whence for Radcliffe-Brown four 'principles': the simple cognatic principle, the principles of 'father-right' and 'mother-right', and the principle of double unilineal descent. In English, cognates are consanguines in general, indifferently paternal (agnates) or maternal (uterine kin). The 'cognatic principle' corresponds to what French, following Lévi-Strauss, calls *systèmes indifférenciés*. In this case we can only speak of descent in a very broad sense. Thus it is that Radcliffe-Brown, when later recapitulating his types (ibid., p. 79), characterises this as the absence of unilineal descent (i.e. descent in the restricted and most usual sense of the term; see below, §§11ff.).

Radcliffe-Brown gives some detailed examples of these different types. For example, 'mother-right' is represented by the Nayar in south India, an extreme case of strict matrilineality. In emphasising descent, he insists on what he calls the 'jural' element. This word is difficult to translate into French. We shall see that it does not mean simply 'legal' or 'juridical'. It concerns relationships that 'can be defined in terms of [customary, LD] rights and duties' (ibid., p. 11), whether there is a legal sanction or only a moral sanction possibly being supplemented by a religious sanction (ibid.). It is a matter, in short, of relationships that are the object of precise, formal prescriptions, whether concerning people or things. Now it is precisely the case, as the author insists, that strictly unilineal systems, whether patrilineal or matrilineal, tend to attach this jural or strictly prescriptive character to relationships within the corresponding line. Thus in a patrilineal system the relationship between father and son is a matter of right and of strictly regulated interest, while, in opposition to this, the relationship between maternal uncle and uterine nephew, free of this aspect to some extent, is characterised by a freer relationship in which affection takes the place of obligation or interest. It is the reverse in matrilineal systems, Radcliffe-Brown insists (ibid., p. 78). Here, though the author does not say so, is a complementarity between two sorts of relationship, a 'structural principle' of systems with stressed unilinearity.

It is clear, however, that on the whole Radcliffe-Brown sees in descent the central and, if not unique, at least predominant principle of kinship systems. It is easy to see what led him to it historically. For a long time special attention had been given, clearly or not, to the mode of descent, which had brought into the limelight the case of the Nayar, for example. Indeed, the 'Introduction' of 1950 and the then master of British anthropology must be granted a special place in the study of lineage systems, one which has been so brilliantly developed by his pupils during the past decade.

This privileged interest corresponds to two facts: (1) the principle of descent is constitutive of social *groups*; (2) as we have seen, what is 'jural' is precise and articulated, and corresponds to the distribution and transmission of goods, as well as the conduct of the most perceptible and restricted relationships between individuals. It is not only this that is important, but, from the empiricist point of view, do we not have here the essence of social relations, the heart of 'social structure'? All this will be appreciated better in what follows, but here, I believe, is what one must read behind the above quotation from Radcliffe-Brown.

The word 'structure' designates something entirely different for Lévi-Strauss, who, in work contemporary with Radcliffe-Brown's 'Introduction', far from privileging any one aspect of kinship, asks on the contrary which necessary relationships unite the mode of descent with other aspects on the same level (residence, marriage rule). We shall return to this in Part III.

PART II

THE THEORY OF UNILINEAL DESCENT GROUPS

D. BEFORE *THE NUER*

11. Descent according to Rivers

Radcliffe-Brown's 'Introduction' in itself shows the very special importance that is attached to descent in British anthropology. The idea is
central to it, among other things because of the development of and
place accorded to the theory of descent groups. Before examining the
latter, it is therefore necessary to understand what is meant by descent.

Linguistically, the overall impression that emerges from the literature is that English says 'descent' where French says *filiation*.[1] Certainly English also has the word 'filiation', but it is of more recent
origin than 'descent'. It even has 'affiliation' in the etymological sense
of 'incorporation in the capacity of a son', which French unfortunately lacks. But until quite recently, as we shall see, English 'filiation'
does not seem to have been used in anthropology, at any rate not by
Radcliffe-Brown, nor in *Notes and Queries*, nor by Evans-Pritchard. We
saw above that it was not used to designate the relationship between
parents and children (§§1–2).

The word 'descent' has a history in British anthropology, and even
though we propose to study its meaning mainly in the works of Radcliffe-Brown and his successors, it is still necessary to go back to Rivers.
In effect, Rivers tried to restrict the anthropological meaning of the
term by applying it to one well-established fact which he regarded as
important. He strove to distinguish clearly, using different terms, distinct institutions or processes that he thought had frequently been
confused: alongside inheritance, residence, and succession or the
transmission of the burdens or functions of authority in a given
group, he put at the head of his list what he called 'descent', i.e. the
transmission of group membership (*Social Organization*, p. 85). Here is
a concise version of what he had to say about it in a 1915 dictionary
article on 'mother-right' (bibliog. no. 6a):

---

[1] This view is challenged by the recent trend which sees itself returning to an earlier usage in
proposing to talk of *descendance*.

Descent: This term should be limited to the process which regulates membership of the social group, such as clan, caste, family, etc. In mother-right descent is matrilineal; [...] *The use of the term is most appropriate when the community is divided into distinct social groups, and this distinctiveness is most pronounced in the clan-organization in which the practice of exogamy separates the social groups called clans clearly from one another.* The social organizations based on the family or kindred are made up of social groups less clearly distinguishable from one another, and, though we may speak of descent in the family whether in the limited or extended sense, the term is here less appropriate. (p. 851a, my emphasis)

I have emphasised one sentence to be kept particularly in mind. In his *Social Organization* (1926), Rivers is even more categorical (bibliog. no. 6b):

We speak of descent as patrilineal when a child belongs to the social group of his father, and as matrilineal when he belongs to the social group of his mother. [...] [T]he use of the term is only of value when the group is unilateral. Therefore, the groups to which it applies most definitely are the clan and the moiety, where, *owing to the principle of exogamy*, a child must belong to the group of the father or mother, but cannot belong to both. The use of the term has little sense, and consequently little value, in the case of the bilateral grouping, of which the *taviti* of the Solomon Islands is so good an example, for this group includes relatives on the sides of both father and mother; the like will hold good in general of the social groups I call kindreds. (p. 86, my emphasis)

Two aspects to be noted are that, following Rivers: (1) the term 'descent' is applied to the automatic transmission of membership in a social group, and that the term only makes sense, or only completely, where the community is composed of absolutely distinct groups (and not of indistinct groupings or groups which overlap); (2) that such is the case essentially with exogamous clans, exogamy ensuring (see the words I have underlined) this absolute distinction and corresponding to unilineality of transmission (patrilineal or matrilineal).

In a recent article, E.R. Leach has very clearly contrasted the meaning given by Rivers to 'descent' with *filiation* in the general French meaning of the term:

Rivers's position implies that a sharp distinction must be made between the notion of 'filiation' or 'pedigree' by which an individual can establish a step-by-step relationship with any one of a great variety of ancestors – e.g. my relationship to my father's mother's father's mother – and the notion of descent which refers to the unambiguous permanent and involuntary membership of a sectional grouping within the total society. ('Unconsidered Aspects', p. 131a, bibliog. no. 7)

Following on from Rivers's definition, one aspect of subsequent evolution might be predicted from a general trend in the anthropological lexicon. In effect, there has been a tendency for many terms ('totem', 'taboo', etc.) to have their meanings extended up to the point where they become useless because they no longer signify anything precise. This has been the case with 'descent', all the more so since Rivers himself did not absolutely exclude the use of the term for groups less strictly defined in relation to one another than exogamous clans. Another, no longer general but specific aspect of the dominant trend has been to minimise or forget the role of exogamy, even when insisting on preserving Rivers's emphasis on the necessary distinction of the groups to which the term is being applied. This last feature is present even in Leach's formula just quoted, though elsewhere this author devotes a lot of space to marriage rules.

Before going further, we must try to translate the term 'descent' into French. This is difficult, which is why I have retained it thus far. The usual French term is *filiation*, and the English 'unilineal descent' is generally translated into French as *filiation unilinéaire*. Thus, in this use of the word, *filiation* takes on a new meaning: the 'transmission of group membership (etc.)'. This situation is due to the fact that French has only one term where English has two: 'filiation' and 'descent'. Obviously this is not a satisfactory situation. Sometimes it is proposed to translate 'descent' by *descendance*, but it would then be hard to preserve the essence of Rivers's meaning. Faced with the lack of any obviously fitting word, one can avoid the ambiguity involved here by introducing *unifiliation* defined as 'descent' in its narrower sense above, where it is always unilineal (see below). There is no inconvenience involved for our present purposes in not being able to translate 'descent' in its less specific senses into French, and it can therefore be retained as it is.

12. 'Descent' and 'Succession' in Radcliffe-Brown

We now come to Radcliffe-Brown. In his 1924 article on the maternal uncle, he speaks of descent entirely in Rivers's sense. It may be either paternal or patrilineal, or maternal or matrilineal; in the patrilineal case, 'the children belong to the group of the father' (*Structure and Function*, p. 22). It is necessary to say a word on his 1935 article on 'Patrilineal and Matrilineal Succession', for it is a classic, and in the words of Meyer Fortes, it is from this 'famous' text that British anthropologists have taken their 'analytic principles' (*Man*, 1959, no. 309, p. 2a, bibliog. no. 11). It is not the category of 'descent' that is to the fore here but that of 'succession', in broader sense than what Rivers meant by it, since it concerns 'the transmission of rights in general' (*Structure and Function*, p. 32). Very briefly, rights, and in particular rights over persons, need to be defined with 'functional consistency' (p. 43), and their transmission must be defined so as to ensure the permanence of the society beyond the unceasing reproduction of individuals. The transmission of rights determined exclusively in a single line, whether paternal or maternal, represents a general solution to the 'problem relating to the determination of status' (p. 39) of each individual, status being defined as the 'totality of all his rights and duties' (p. 37) (each right evidently having a correlative duty). The continuity with respect to Rivers becomes clear when Radcliffe-Brown writes that the system of succession turns to a large extent around the system of marriage, jurally privileging the tie between brother and sister at the expense of that between husband and wife (the matrilineal Nayar) or inversely (the patrilineal Romans) (p. 42), as he says, a little differently, in his later 'Introduction' (see above, §9, at end). More immediately evocative of Rivers is the passage in which he says that one can easily imagine a local community possessing individual rights over things and being completely endogamous, but in which the question of unilineal succession arises as soon as there is intermarriage between two local groups of this sort (p. 46). Meyer Fortes summarises Radcliffe-Brown's article in 1955 as follows:

> What [the author] demonstrates is that 'matriliny' and 'patriliny' are simply alternative ways of reaching a solution of the fundamental problem of succession...: to determine unequivocally where rights over persons reside and to stabilize these rights. (*British Journal of Sociology*, VI/1, p. 21)

Here, the disciple definitely if imperceptibly goes beyond the master. Everything depends on the little word 'simply': the one thing that is truly essential in any society is the definition and transmission of rights and, by consequence, unilineal descent. Exogamy and marriage, which for Radcliffe-Brown were still social institutions in the full sense, are no longer for Fortes anything more than secondary aspects external to the 'kinship structure' proper, as is confirmed clearly in an adjacent passage: 'both prohibited and preferential marriages must be analysed with reference to the effect they have in preserving and maintaining an existing kinship structure' (ibid., p. 22).

If we turn to the 'Introduction' of 1950 (especially p. 13, already quoted above, §10), we see that Radcliffe-Brown here combines two distinct elements under the word 'descent': on the one hand descent in the widest sense of the term, and on the other the formal or jural aspect, which he had previously described under the term 'succession'. In both cases, we have now come a long way from Rivers. If not on page 79, at least on page 13 (as pointed out above), Radcliffe-Brown opposes four major types of kinship system from the point of view of descent, of which one, that founded on the 'simple cognatic principle', is characterised precisely by the absence of unilineal descent (the other three being founded on unilineal descent, whether paternal, maternal or double). Even the expression 'unilineal descent' has a very wide sense here (p. 14), designating the recognition of kinship in the single line (paternal or maternal) more or less emphasised by the particular society, the 'formation of recognized lineage groups' being only one 'important way in which [it] may be used'. I therefore conclude that for Radcliffe-Brown, at any rate in 1950, 'descent' concerns above all the transmission of rights and duties (and the organisation of these rights and duties between different generations). This aspect corresponds to a great extent, though not absolutely, to Rivers' transmission of membership in the unilineal descent group, wherever such a group exists. As Meyer Fortes says:

> Radcliffe-Brown's concept of descent [is] fundamentally a jural or legal notion that *inter alia* regulates the forms of grouping [concerning] corporate 'ownership'. (*British Journal of Sociology*, VI/1, p. 22) ['corporate' meaning 'indivisible property which makes a group a moral person', LD]

This formulation, proposed with respect to the study of political systems, is certainly tendentious: it would apply rather badly to the case of the Nuer, for example. But, in its insistence on property, it expresses at the very least a powerful, if not predominant trend among the successors of Radcliffe-Brown. It is, moreover, perfectly clear as to the subordination of group membership not only to the 'economic' reality of the group, but above all to the definition and transmission of individual rights and duties. With this last point, we are certainly dealing with a predominant theme in British anthropology.

The development with respect to Rivers is therefore very clear, and we shall clarify it further below (§20).

Personal Commentary

Let us pause for a moment with this idea of 'rights and duties' and the place accorded to it. We think we notice an ambiguity to begin with: this idea tends to bring the individual to the fore, the subject of these rights and duties; yet at the same time indivisibility is stressed, where the rights of the individual are, so to say, merged with those of the group. In reality these are two aspects of the same fact: one isolates a physical or *moral* person as the subject of the right. The method is certainly convenient: it allows us to stay as close as possible to modern jural concepts. But we may wonder precisely if this is really what is required: is law in the societies studied the same as ours in this respect? Can we reasonably express the multitude of usages that limit the properly jural sphere in the strictly individualistic language of Bentham, in whose writings the whole society is hardly expressed except in the language of utility?

In our own civilisation, the subjective concept of law, to which is attached the concept of the 'rights and duties' of the individual, has succeeded an objective concept, according to which law is that which conforms to order. The latter concept, ideal and realist by opposition to the positivism and nominalism of the modern one, is, judging by what we know, likely to be infinitely closer to those concepts which are generally current in non-modern societies. It should permit one to pay much more attention to all the nuances of interdependence by which a man in a particular role is to some extent merged in a vaster subject, yet without his being dissolved in it entirely. The concept of 'rights and duties' implicitly supposes that the modern idea of the individual can be extended to tribal or traditional societies, but such an extension must often produce a serious distortion of the given society. It would not be difficult to give examples of this from India and south Asia. The understanding of the world of castes is much easier from other points of view. For example, I have proposed replacing the individual subject there with a subject formed of a pair of complementarities (*Civilisation indienne et nous*, pp. 21ff.). More generally, the modern concept of the individual contains a very special normative element (see my *Homo Hierarchicus*, §3, and, for the beginnings of a juridical subjectivity, *Contributions to Indian Sociology*, VIII, pp. 18ff., summarising Michel Villey, 'La Formation de la pensée juridique moderne').

13. Unilineal Descent and Other Modes of Descent

Our principal aim here is the study of 'descent groups', in actual fact unilineal descent groups, in British anthropology. In everything that follows, therefore, and without inconvenience, we can take 'descent' in the restricted meaning of Rivers and Leach and translate the term into French as *unifiliation*. I shall not deal with cognatic systems, to which certain authors apply the term 'descent', since group membership does not automatically result from birth (the possibility of choice) and since these groups are not mutually exclusive, as Rivers required them to be and as is the case with unilineal groups. These questions actually seem confused enough to me, and in any case they are not part of the central contribution of English anthropology (see Leach, 'Unconsidered Aspects', column 131a, bibliog. no. 7).

I shall simply note that, in contrast to Rivers's usage, Radcliffe-Brown's, about which Leach curiously says not a word, inevitably leads its adherents to speak of 'descent' even in those cases ruled out by Rivers. In fact, cognatic systems too involve simultaneously the existence of modes of distributing and transmitting rights, and local communities. To the extent that stress is placed on these aspects, it is natural in practice to speak of 'descent' in all societies. In this perspective, the existence of exclusive groups linked among themselves by exogamy tends to become blurred.[2]

---

[2] In this connection, it will be noted that the 'Esquisse d'un glossaire de la parenté' [Sketch of a Kinship Glossary], prepared by the Cercle des Jeunes Anthropologues and published in their bulletin *L'Échange*, no. 7, May 1966, is far more aimed at cognatic systems than being concerned with kinship in general or with its better-known forms.

E. EVANS-PRITCHARD: *THE NUER*

14. *The Nuer*: Structural Relativity

It would be a waste of time trying to summarise here Evans-Pritchard's major work, *The Nuer: A Description of the Modes of Livelihood and Political Institutions of a Nilotic People* (bibliog. no. 8). A masterpiece of modern monographic literature, it could not be more condensed. Instead of attempting to summarise it, it is better to try and define its original contribution in brief. Above all, the work constitutes the foundation of the theory of political systems and unilineal descent groups in British anthropology. It represents at once a continuity with and a break from Radcliffe-Brown (D.F. Pocock, *Social Anthropology*).[3] Here are the aspects which we must bring out to begin with. The most general feature, one which characterises the book from end to end and opposes it to its predecessors – and even to many of its successors – is its structural aspect: Evans-Pritchard considerably deepened Radcliffe-Brown's idea of 'social structure'. But it is not enough to say this, for he replaced this vague notion with a precise idea which is really that of 'structure' in the strict sense of the term, as I shall attempt to show.

We might start by insisting on the 'relativity' of ideas, a topic to which Evans-Pritchard often returned and which he had already placed at the heart of his great book, *Witchcraft, Oracles and Magic Among the Azande* (Oxford, 1937). Concerning local groups, or local communities, we are told that, in employing such and such a name to designate them, the Nuer is 'identifying himself with a local community, and, *by so doing, cutting himself off from other communities of the same kind*' (*The Nuer*, p. 135, my emphasis). The author adds: 'An examination of the word *cieng* will teach us one of the most fundamental characters of Nuer local groups and, indeed, of all social groups: their structural relativity' (ibid.).

---

[3] Quotations and references can be found in my Preface to the French translation of *The Nuer*, Gallimard 1968, from which I have taken the conclusions of the present study [English translation of Preface 1975; see second bibliography, RP.]

What does a Nuer mean when he says, 'I am a man of such-and-such a *cieng*'? *Cieng* means 'home', but its precise significance varies with the situation in which it is spoken. If one meets an Englishman in Germany and asks him where his home is, he may reply that it is England. If one meets the same man in London and asks him the same question he will tell one that his home is in Oxfordshire, whereas if one meets him in that county he will tell one the name of the town or village in which he lives. [...] So it is with the Nuer. A Nuer met outside Nuerland says that his home is *cieng Nath*, Nuerland. He may also refer to his tribal country as his *cieng*, though the more usual expression for this is *rol*. If one asks him in his tribe what is his *cieng*, he will name his village or tribal section according to the context. Generally he will name either his tertiary tribal section or his village, but he may give his primary or secondary section. If asked in his village he will mention the name of his hamlet or indicate his homestead or the end of the village in which his homestead is situated. Hence if a man says 'Wa ciengda', 'I am going home', outside his village he means that he is returning to it, if in his village he means that he is going to his hamlet, if in his hamlet he means that he is going to his homestead. *Cieng* thus means homestead, hamlet, village, and tribal sections of various dimensions. (*Nuer*, p. 136)

The author adds that these variations in the meaning of the word are not due to linguistic incoherence, but to the relativity of the groups (more exactly, of the 'group-values') to which the word refers. This relativity must be understood in order that 'the apparent contradictions in our account will be seen to be contradictions in the structure itself, being, in fact, a quality of it'. Here is a transition: it is clear that we are no longer at the level of Radcliffe-Brown's 'social structure', but well and truly at the level of structure in the strict and intellectual sense of the term, of structure as a system of oppositions.

What is involved is the relativity of elements in a segmentary system, and this is true of the political system, the lineage system and the age-class system indifferently. Let there be a system of groups in which the groups A, B, C, D, etc., comprise subdivisions of the first order A1, A2, A3, B1, B2, B3, etc., these in their turn comprising subdivisions of the second order A1a, A1b, etc., B1a, B1b, etc., and so on. Let us stop at the third order: A1a1, etc.[4] *The system is said to be segmentary if the subdivisions of the different orders* potentially co-exist at any instant but only manifest themselves by turns in specific situations. Let us take territorial groups as an illustration.

---

[4] It has not been considered necessary to remain faithful to the author's representation, which is not very clear and on at least one occasion ambiguous ('A,B,C', pp. 193, 201). I have preferred a representation which translates the author's ideas more clearly and systematically.

Let us suppose that a member of A1a1 has committed a murder. Three possibilities present themselves, depending on whether the victim is a member of A2 by opposition to A1, of A1c by opposition to A1a, or of A1a*n* by opposition to A1a1 (see Fig. 1).

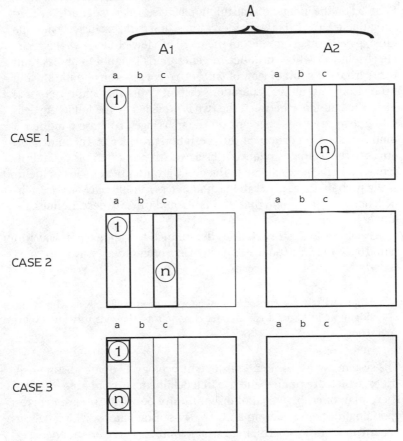

Figure 1.

Case 1: The victim is a member of A2c*n*: the whole of A2 is united against the whole of A1. The conflict is between subdivisions of the first order.

Case 2: The victim is a member of A1c*n*: the whole of A1c is united against the whole of A1a. The conflict is between subdivisions of the second order.

Case 3: The victim is a member of A1a*n*: the conflict is between A1a1 and A1a*n*, subdivisions of the third order.

15. *The Nuer*: Political System and Lineage System

We have seen (§§5–6) that Evans-Pritchard distinguishes, besides the family, three different 'systems': the kinship system, the lineage system and the political system. The distinction between the first two is founded on the indigenous distinction between *mar*, 'cognatic' or con-sanguineal kinship between individuals, and *buth*, exclusively agnatic kinship between groups. From the point of view of *mar*, ego has a cir-cle of relatives whose distance in generations is equal to or less than three; from the point of view of *buth*, ego recognises an agnatic kinship group from four or five generations distant. From this agnatic point of view, the boundary between the two is provided by the following defi-nition: *mar* are 'those persons on the marriage of whose daughter a man can claim a portion' of the prestation provided by the man's rel-atives to the woman's relatives ('bridewealth proper'). This extends in reality (and reciprocally) up to the great-grandfather of the girl inclu-sively, perhaps three generations of agnates (*Kinship and Marriage*, bib-liog. no. 9, p. 7). Beyond that, *mar* ends, and we have descent lines, no longer individuals.

Elsewhere, Evans-Pritchard is determined to isolate a political sys-tem. The 'political structure' is defined in a preliminary way at the out-set (*The Nuer*, p. 4); it concerns

> relations within a territorial system between groups of persons who live in spatially well-defined areas and are conscious of their identity and exclu-siveness.

The system has a close relationship with ecology. The Nuer distinguish tribes, which are named and live in a definite territorial area, though there may often be a spatial discontinuity between the area corre-sponding to the wet season and the dry-season camps, which collect around more or less permanent water sources. There are neither spe-cialised political organs nor any permanent political authority, not even at the level of the tribe or its sub-divisions. The Nuer have no state, unless it is a 'state of kinship'; they live in what we would literally have to call anarchy, but it is an 'ordered anarchy' (p. 181, etc.), and it is this anarchic order whose principles the author wishes to grasp in isolating what he calls the Nuer 'political system'. It can certainly be said that the principle of this relative order is a double one: on the one hand, it consists in the segmentary or structural character of the ter-ritorial subdivisions of the tribes, which simultaneously brings them together and separates them from one another, maintaining in short a 'structural distance' between them; on the other hand, it consists in the clans and lineages which provide the 'conceptual skeleton' (p. 212) of these territorial units, as will be seen in what follows.

The author distinguishes 'tribal sections' or subdivisions of three successive orders: primary, secondary and tertiary. The tribe, which we shall call Σa, is thus subdivided into a1, a2, a3 primary tribal sections, these in their turn into secondary sections: a1.1, a1.2, etc., a2.1, a2.2, etc.; and these into tertiary sections: a1.1.1, a1.1.2, a1.2.2, etc.

Parallel with this, in the lineage system, clan ΣA is divided into 'maximal' lineages, A1, A2, A3, these maximal lineages into 'major' lineages, A1.1, A1.2, etc., A2.1, A2.2, etc.; and the major lineages into 'minor' lineages, A1.1.1, A1.1.2, etc., A1.2.1, A1.2.2, etc. Finally, the 'minor' lineages are subdivided into 'minimal' lineages, which we will leave aside here.

There is a correspondence between these two segmentary wholes, for:

1. One *patrilineal* group is always dominant within a specific *territorial* group, i.e., to simplify a little, one clan within the tribe, one maximal lineage (A1) in the primary tribal section (a1), etc.
2. While the tribe (Σa) and the clan (ΣA) have distinct names, it is not the same at the level of the subdivisions, where it is the *dominant patrilineal group that gives its name to the corresponding territorial section.* This is the case most of the time, if not always, which leads the author to write the same proper name in small capitals when he is designating a patrilineal group, and in lower case letters when he is designating the territorial group in which this patrilineal group is dominant. It is for this reason that I have here chosen symbols such that the territorial unit appears to correspond to the patrilineal group which gives it its name (say, the secondary tribal section a1.1 and the major lineage A1.1). Whence the following diagram (Fig. 2):

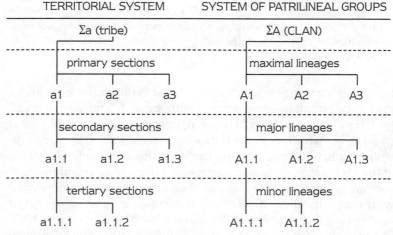

Figure 2.

16. *The Nuer*: Clarifications and Explanations

The ideal scheme that has just been hazarded requires a certain number of clarifications and explanations to make complete sense. To start
with, to say 'clan' is not to say 'dominance within the tribe', for two
main reasons (p. 213): (1) not all clans have a superior or 'dominant'
status within the tribe: there are some clans that are not dominant
anywhere, and some descent lines of Dinka origin are absorbed, as
subordinate ones, into the territorial network; (2) not all members of a
clan live where the clan is dominant, for, in contrast with the tribes,
the clans are *dispersed* throughout Nuer country; wherever my clan is
dominant, I have aristocratic status (*dil*); wherever it is not, I have the
status of a stranger (*rul*) in relation to the dominant aristocrats. Let us
quote in its entirety a paragraph in which the character of the relationships between descent lines and territorial groups is admirably
indicated:

> Nuer lineages are not corporate, localized, communities [i.e. collectivities
> which, because of their relationship with the soil, constitute moral per-
> sons, LD], though they are frequently associated with territorial units, and
> those members of a lineage who live in an area associated with it see them-
> selves as a residential group, and [ultimately] the value, or concept, of lin-
> eage thus functions through the political system. Every Nuer village is
> associated with a lineage, and, though the members of it often constitute
> only a small proportion of the village population, the village community is
> identified with them in such a way that we may speak of it as an aggregate
> of persons clustered around an agnatic nucleus. The aggregate is linguisti-
> cally identified with the nucleus by the common designation of the village
> community by the name of the lineage. It is only in reference to rules of
> exogamy, certain ritual activities, and to a very limited extent to responsi-
> bility for homicide, that one needs to regard lineages as completely
> autonomous groups. In social life generally they function within local com-
> munities, of all sizes from the village to the tribe, and as part of them.
> (*Nuer*, p. 203)

It is exactly that lineage which is recognised as the core of a territorial
group and gives it its name that the author calls a 'dominant lineage'
(p. 205). This is most likely to concern the first occupants of the region
(p. 212), but what is essential is that they are considered to have a pre-
eminent and unique tie with this territory. This 'dominance' is defined
at the level of the tribe in its entirety, and 'in each tribe a clan, *or a maximal lineage* [NB, in respect of our ideal scheme, LD] ... is associated
with the political group in which it occupies a dominant position
among the other dominant groups that live within it ... [and] each of
its segments [of this clan or lineage, LD] *tends* [NB] to be associated'

with the segments of the tribe (pp. 211–12, my emphases). The author translates as 'aristocrat' the Nuer term (*dil*, plural *diel*) that indicates this superior status by opposition to *rul*, stranger, which is applied to the other lineages or lineage segments. Moreover, it is more a matter of prestige and influence than of rank and power (p. 215), for the Nuer have strongly egalitarian tendencies. The difference is only significant in the calculation of 'blood-cattle', i.e. in the number of animals to be given up in compensation for a homicide if the murder took place within a unit in which the difference of status is pertinent, i.e. the village (for example, 20 animals instead of 17 in recent times). Conversely, in relation to other segments in other villages, the difference between *dil* and *rul* is neutralized: there is no differentiation within a political segment in relation to other segments.

It is the same for the status below the two preceding ones, that of *jaang*, which is applied to an adult or unadopted captive Dinka (see below) in contrast to a locally born Dinka. One is *jaang* only within the Nuer family to which one is attached; from the outside, one is simply a member of that family (p. 219). Just as the groups are relative one to another, so is status relative to the groups.

Let us refine what has been said relating to the designation of the territorial unit by means of the name of the corresponding patrilineal group. This applies in general (for example, pp. 204–5), but not always. In particular, the tribes, and sometimes their primary sections, have their own names, and it is the same with villages, which have place names, even though they can also be designated by the name of their 'principal lineage'. Let us take particular note of this last expression, which indicates that the principal lineage in a village might not form part of the dominant clan within the tribe: the site of the village then does not belong to it but by custom to the dominant clan, which is why a special term is needed to designate such a lineage (p. 207 n.).

Finally, in closing his chapter on 'The Lineage System', Evans-Pritchard makes considerably more precise the relationship between lineage segmentation and political segmentation. It would be straining his meaning to say that the second is the cause of the first, but at least it governs it to a large extent: the segmentation of descent lines follows the territorial segmentation; the 'lineage structure is twisted into the form of the political structure' (p. 241). The author gives examples and various proofs of this, including the following: 'the range of counting agnation is largely determined by its organizing role in the political structure' (p. 246):

> As we understand the process, what happens is that certain lineage groups
> gain political importance and exclusiveness, becoming nuclei of tribal sec-
> tions, and that only by doing so is their structural position stabilized and

are the points of their bifurcation rendered fixed and permanent points of convergence in lineage structure. This explains how it is that in only a few out of a vast number of polygamous families is maternal descent structurally significant, and why bifurcation occurs in the lineage where it occurs in the tribe. (p. 247)

17. *The Nuer*: Mode of Correspondence between the Political System and the Lineage System

We shall understand the foregoing better when we see how the correspondence between the two systems is actually established. There are three ways, of increasing scope: adoption, through which an adolescent captive Dinka is incorporated into the Nuer lineage that has captured him; intermarriage, which results in the establishment of ties of consanguinity between members of different descent lines within local communities; and finally myths, which unite the largest patrilineal and even territorial units.

There is little to be said about adoption: it is a matter of adoption within the lineage (and thus naturally of incorporation within the family), which can only be applied to young male captive Dinka, not to adults (whence the inevitable existence of Dinka lineages) nor to Nuer (for a Nuer cannot change lineage). The adopted Dinka is purely and simply grafted on to the Nuer lineage, and his descendants will trace their ancestry back to the Nuer ancestor of the descent line [*lignée*]. The Dinka is, in short, wholly absorbed into the Nuer lineage.

The Nuer clan is exogamous, and there is even a prohibition on marriage into one's mother's maximal lineage (by contrast, an adopted Dinka can marry into the collateral lineage of the clan of his adoptive lineage):

> Nuer rules of exogamy break down the exclusiveness of agnatic groups by compelling their members to marry outside them, and thereby to create new kinship ties. (p. 225)

This is a remarkable formulation. We might be content with finding within it a reminder, or a confirmation, of Rivers's concept of unilineal descent, in which the existence of unilineal groups is tied to exogamy. But it is precisely with respect to the complementarity posed by Rivers between perfectly distinct groups on the one hand and relations of intermarriage necessarily external to these groups on the other that Evans-Pritchard's formulation is somewhat surprising: save for brief allusions, intermarriage is not considered in this light in the first 224 pages of the book, while from Ch. 4 (p. 139) interest is concentrated on political and agnatic groups, which are certainly considered in respect of their relativity, but independently of this essential tie between themselves or their members. However, the importance of the transfers of livestock as marriage prestations ('bridewealth') is made very obvious (see *The Nuer*, Index, s.v.). When we are presented with the 'exclusivity' of agnatic groups which marriage rules are supposed to break down, we are entitled to wonder where this exclusivity is actually situated. To the extent that it is not situated entirely in the mind of the author and is not being intruded as a stylistic procedure for increasing the 'exclusive' attention to groups in themselves, this exclusivity is situated well and truly within the space prescribed for it by exogamy, which does not break it down but enslaves it. In so far as it is inaccurate and overrated, Evans-Pritchard's formulation, when set alongside the view taken by Rivers, brings us face to face with the revolution worked in British anthropology to the benefit of groups and contrary to the sorts of relation which most radically limit them. Although Evans-Pritchard's successors appear to us to have distanced themselves from him in other respects, on this point, on the contrary, he is the precursor of all that will follow. All one can say is that exogamy will often be treated worse than this. But it must be pointed out that one already starts here with *elements* that supposedly have a reality in themselves (territorial, 'corporate' or agnatic) in order to restore the *whole* only at the end. It is the privileged or exclusive attention given to *groups*, more or less as collective subjects or collective individuals, that leads to what must be called a distortion from a structural point of view, a subordination of the relationship between the parts and the whole.

The first consequence of intermarriage is that all the inhabitants of one village are generally related to one another. The 'aggregate' that constitutes the village is an aggregate of relatives grouped around a core constituted by the dominant (or principal) lineage. Certainly these non-agnatic relationships are, by opposition to agnatic ones, personal, not group relationships. However, consanguineal relationships are generalised at the level of local groups or lineages. Indeed, one usually designates non-agnatic relations as 'daughter's children' (*gaat nyiet*) (or should we rather say 'children by daughters'?), which apply between lineages following a single intermarriage. Thus between lineage elements [*éléments lignagers*], and therefore between groups, there are ties of consanguineal (or 'cognatic') kinship, as opposed to the postulated antithesis between *mar* and *buth*. What must be remembered is that, unlike agnatic kinship, consanguinity does not constitute groups.

Since marriage is prohibited not only within the father's clan but also between close consanguines, and even into the whole of the mother's maximal lineage, the network of intermarriage is necessarily extended between different villages and different territorial units.

> Thus the kinship system bridges the gaps in political structure by a chain of links which unite members of opposed elements (p. 226),

which poses 'a set of complex problems' (ibid.). The sole aspect the author retains here is the role played by non-agnatic kinship in the cohesion of territorial units:

> A lineage remains an exclusive group only in ritual situations. In other situations it is merged in the community, and cognation (*mar*) takes the place of lineage agnation (*buth*) as the value through which people living together express their relations to one another. (p. 228)

We have seen that adoption permits the incorporation of young Dinka captives into Nuer descent lines [*lignées*], and that non-agnatic kinship unites people of different agnatic ancestries [*ascendance*] around an agnatic core in territorial communities, in the first place in the village. A third way of securing the conjunction of agnation and territoriality consists in the 'mythological creation of kinship fictions'. This is 'appropriate to relations between dominant lineages and stranger and Dinka groups, living with them in the same tribal segments, which are too large and occupy too distinct a territory for incorporation by either of the other two methods' (p. 228). For example, the Lou tribe has Jinaca as its dominant clan. In regular fashion, three maximal lineages of the Jinaca clan each give their name to a secondary tribal section (NB: not a primary section, as in our theoretical diagram), i.e. Gaaliek, Gaatbal and Rumjok. But this is not all, and two other secondary tribal sections have the maximal lineages Jimac and Jaajoah as the dominant ones, which do not belong to the Jinaca clan. There is a myth accounting for this anomaly. The two descent lines [*lignées*] go back to the sons of sisters: two brothers, who had mysteriously disappeared, were replaced by two sisters (and the myth in question contains more than this, as we shall see). The mythology of the Gaatgankiir clan is far richer. It accounts not merely for the insertion, at the level of the secondary tribal sections, of two heterogeneous lineages into the primary section Reng of the Gaajak tribe, but also for the separation into different tribes of relatively close lineages, and conversely for the coming together in the same tribe of relatively distant lineages. It thus goes beyond what the author had postulated, in so far as the myth transcends the idea of the tribe being determined and established through relationships between different tribes by means of agnatic relationships within the same clan (pp. 231–32).

The matter goes much further: the myths establish relationships between different dominant clans and different tribes, ultimately bringing 'the whole of Nuerland into a single kinship structure' (p. 236). In contrast to the 'lineage system', which is always within a given clan, one would have here a 'clan system' (p. 236). The tribes themselves are personified and placed in relations of kinship. At the limit, the common ancestor or ancestors of all Nuer are named: 'a single kinship or pseudo-kinship system' connects 'all the territorial segments of Nuerland' (p. 240). We see, therefore, on the one hand that, while it constitutes the 'conceptual skeleton' of territorial units, agnatic kinship invokes non-agnatic kinship in a complementary way; and on the other hand that these kinship ties are not, in the final analysis, contained within the framework of territorial units, even the most extensive ones, but on the contrary they encompass them. As the author says at several points: 'Kinship values are the strongest sentiments and norms in Nuer society and all interrelations tend to be expressed in a kinship idiom' (p. 228). In particular, 'community [territorial] relations are translated into kinship relations' (ibid.).

Let us note in passing that this is undoubtedly the prototype of the viewpoint developed by Beattie as regards the nature of kinship (the antithesis between language and content, above, §7). Let us note also that Evans-Pritchard does not develop the idea of what he himself calls the 'clan system', but briefly indicates, at the end of the chapter devoted to the 'lineage system', that this system encompasses Nuer society. We understand that it is a matter here, at the level of the tribe, only of vague representations which do not correspond to fixed features of behaviour: the totality of Nuer tribes, though conceived vaguely from the point of view of such and such a particular tribe, never resides in any acts or ceremonies whatsoever. It is not altogether the same at the level of the clan, for we have seen that patrilineal 'exclusivity' is 'broken down' very effectively by the law of exogamy: every marriage is consequently to some extent a lived relationship between different clans. Finally, the fact of presenting non-agnatic kinship and mythical kinship, whether agnatic or not, as a simple means of establishing relations between agnatic groups and territorial groups cannot fail to appear arbitrary.

This is to a great extent the result of an exclusive attention, or rather privileged emphasis, that is given to 'groups', which relegates relations between these groups to a secondary level when they are neither territorial nor agnatic. The author rigidly considers myths in particular to be rationalisations of privileged relationships (p. 229). The clan ancestor and his male descendants, as lineage ancestors, are not presented as especially mythical, but only their wives and the other mythical circumstances surrounding the foundations of lineages and tribes. In the case cited of the Lou tribe, the ancestor of the Jinaca clan, Denac, has two wives, Nyagun and Nyamor, who give their names to the Gun and Mor primary sections. What makes these two eponymous women any more 'mythical' than their husbands? Moreover, the details contradict the author's thesis that genealogies merely reflect territorial relationships between descent lines. In fact, the Jinaca clan is dominant in two tribes, Lou and Rengyan, with two maximal lineages in the latter. We would expect, therefore, given that there are two wives, that the children of one may be the ancestors of the lineages of the Lou tribe, the others being the ancestors of the Rengyan tribe. But this is not the case: two Lou lineages and two Rengyan lineages are descended from the first wife, one Lou lineage (and the two 'sister's children' lineages, equally Lou) from the second wife.

18. The Idea of Structure in *The Nuer*

Let us try and bring out what is essential about this book. At the start the author, having recalled the formidable difficulties he had to face in his fieldwork, presents his book as 'a contribution to the ethnology' of a region rather than a 'detailed sociological study' (p. 15). This declaration is contradicted by the work overall and by the author himself when, most happily, he summarises his theoretical preoccupations and his 'short excursion into sociological theory' at the end (p. 266). His main theme is political institutions (p. 4). This is a matter of seeing what replaces territorial government among a people who do not possess any, and how an order which is, at the very least, relative prevails where there is literally anarchy. With respect to the plan of the book, the political system is situated at the point of intersection between on the one hand ecology and distribution in space, which, with demography, provides it with its primary matter, and on the other hand the 'lineage system', which gives it its 'conceptual skeleton'. The central preoccupation involves a privileged attention being given to 'groups' (p. 4): indeed, it is the relations between local groups that can be called political (pp. 264–65). The examination is justified in at least two ways. First, in the reciprocal play of territory and kinship in the wider sense of the term, it is the territorial or political aspect which constitutes 'the dominant variable', and 'living together counts for more than kinship' (p. 265); in short, as others would say today (see above, §7), the political 'content' is more important than the 'language' of kinship in which it is usually expressed. The other justification, which also appears clearly in the last pages of the book, is the need to make progress in anthropological theory: in distinguishing special systems like those of kinship (in the restricted sense), lineages or political groups, we pass from the concrete level of groups or 'masses' of people to the level of relations, and of relations between these relations. And indeed, the relation between the 'political system' and the 'lineage system' constitutes the theme of the second part of the book.

However, in his conclusion, the author appears uncertain or perplexed: the relations between systems have still not been presented satisfactorily, he has studied the political aspect in a little-known territory, he is short of supplies, it is for his successors to take things further. They have not failed to do so. What is a system? It is a collection of relations between groups (p. 246). A structure, defined initially as that which endures in a society, is a little different: a collection of personal relationships is not a structure, for, since they do not involve groups, there is nothing permanent, or relatively permanent, in the life of the society. It is necessary to take special note of the paradox in this double stress on 'group' and 'relation'. Real or durable or principal relations would be relations between permanent groups: relations of kinship (or relations between these relations) also transcend the ephemeral individual subject, but they do not reach the pre-eminent status that group relations attain in a system of groups. And yet the author's essential contribution will consist in destroying these substances, in demonstrating their 'structural relativity'. A strange paradox. We realise fully that it is the attention given to politics that imposes this, as it were. But conversely, why the choice of the political dimension, if not by virtue of this substantialist apriorism?

It is characteristic that the doubts and scruples expressed by the author in his conclusion leave the choice of the political dimension absolutely intact. It is impossible for us to explain this choice: the particular circumstances of the enquiry, the author's ideological preferences and development, and the collective preoccupations of the British anthropological environment of the 1930s all escape us to a large extent. The teaching of Radcliffe-Brown, as perceptible in many of the aspects of the Nuer as it is contradicted or superseded in others, is less directly informative here than the very posterity of the Nuer. It is clear that Evans-Pritchard opened a way that had been expected, one in which the whole of British anthropology has engulfed itself since. We shall see in the following section what is relative and structural for our author becoming hardened and solidified. But here precisely is an indication that his innovation is not purely an individual one. What is personal to him is the passage from group to relation, its relativisation.

This fact prompts me to ask the reader's permission to speculate a little further, as a way of warning him that what follows is necessarily less scientific than what precedes. It will also inevitably be 'personal' in the sense that we shall be moving away from perspectives that are currently accepted in contemporary anthropology.

Let us do, therefore, what posterity has not yet done and bring into question this way of treating the political dimension.[5] Is there really a political system among the Nuer? Lest we raise questions that are too general, let us pose a question that is more limited: is there any point in distinguishing the political 'system' and the lineage 'system' from each other? In my account, what is most often in question in the two corresponding chapters is the *correspondence* between the two 'systems' (cf. *Kinship and Marriage*, bibliog. no. 9, p. 1). It is far from being my intention to deny that there is a territorial *dimension* in the Nuer politico-lineage system, and that it is territorial groups, as distinct from lineage groupings, that correspond to this dimension. But what profound interest is there in erecting the two sorts of group into two distinct systems if we no longer think in terms of 'masses' but of relations? The so-called political system has neither head nor tongue: it is expressed almost entirely in the language of clans, lineages and ancestral myths. All the tension which exists between the two 'systems' comes from this: the presumed dominant variable constantly makes use of a spokesman to explain itself, and inversely – care is taken to draw this frequently to our attention – the lineage spokesman is very rarely occupied in speaking on his own behalf (ritual situations). In short, to separate the two systems is to separate 'content' and 'form'. Would it not be better to reunite them? We would then recognise simply that the collection of lineages, and beyond it that of the clans, somewhat neglected here, has a political function, and examine how the political dimension, far from being independent, is here an attribute of the system of patrilineal groups.[6] We could then compare it with societies in which the variable is independent and with other societies in which the same function can be served otherwise. All the positive contribution of *The Nuer* would remain, and more attention could be devoted to the non-agnatic aspects of kinship, whether as the complement of agnation within territorial units (for a precise relation of complementary must exist), or whether outside them. Would the close identifica-

---

[5] The opposite has been proposed by M.G Smith, 'On Segmentary Lineage Systems', *Journal of the Royal Anthropological Institute*, LXXXVI/2, 1956, pp. 39–80.

[6] In an article unknown to me at the time of preparing this analysis, Marshall D. Sahlins revives this question: the *segmentary* system of lineages is accounted for by the Nuer's aggressive relations with their neighbours, the relation in the centre governs (this aspect of) its internal organisation. 'The Segmentary Lineage: An Organization of Predatory Expansion', *American Anthropologist*, LXIII, 1961, pp. 322–45.

tion of the Nuer with his ox be possible if the ox only symbolised the permanence of the lineage, and not also and at the same time, though more implicitly, matrimonial exchanges, i.e. in the last analysis two complementary aspects of kinship?

Willy-nilly, we are forced to conclude that at the global level the treatment of the Nuer is not structural in the sense of an anthropology going from the whole to the parts and putting the relation before the terms of the relation. It moves away from the territorial group or the lineage group as a collective individual in restoring relations of a different order (kinship, non-agnatic kinship) in which the group is caught up. Evans-Pritchard's successors will not do this to the same extent. This being so, it is no less remarkable to see a truly structuralist perspective being established at the level of these groups themselves: they appear and disappear according to situations, they are caught up in a never-ending movement of fission and fusion – equally relative, temporary when taken separately, but constant in their totality – and it is this 'elasticity' which permits the order to exist, it being understood that it is based on a collection of common representations without which it would be impossible. And this is not only a matter of fact: some of the passages we have quoted show that conceptually groups only exist in their relative situation, when opposed to one another. We can speak of segmentation in order to designate the particular sort of structure which opposes entities of the same nature. It will be noted that this is not the most durable aspect of British anthropology, though it is still more precious: it is Evans-Pritchard's own contribution, as opposed to what he shares with his immediate contemporaries.

Let us conclude with a later passage by the author himself (*Kinship and Marriage*, 'Conclusion', pp. 176–77):

> Thus members of the same lineage are bound to each other by common descent, by ritual ties, by common cattle-interests, by the duty of blood-revenge and other moral obligations, by association with a common territory, and so forth, while they are united within the wider society to persons, and as a group to other lineages, by multiple ties of kinship, all of which lack the ambivalence of agnatic kinship. We have noted, moreover, that the Nuer lineage is not merely a descent group but is a descent group with political functions. It may not therefore be too fanciful to suggest that the agnatic type of kin relationships is associated with the autonomy of political segments and their structural opposition to one another – the process of fission, and the non-agnatic type of kin relationships is associated, through a complex network of ties of this type, with the wider social system which binds these segments together and contains them – the process of fusion. The one set of attitudes emphasizes the singularity and exclusiveness of the agnatic group...the other...the community life in which such groups are merged.

F. AFTER *THE NUER*

19. Meyer Fortes

Since we cannot follow the theory of descent groups throughout British anthropology, I shall briefly consider a trend of particular interest, one associated with the Cambridge school of anthropology represented principally by Meyer Fortes. The name of Meyer Fortes is linked to the invention of what he has called 'complementary filiation', but in order to understand and situate this idea correctly, it is necessary to take into account the author's theory in general. He sums up the whole British development clearly in an article on 'The Structure of Unilineal Descent Groups', which reproduces a conference paper given to the American Anthropological Association in 1951 (bibliog. no. 10).

Its first striking feature is the importance accorded to the search for an 'order of priority' in the interdependence of institutions (p. 21). This concerns the 'problem of assigning an order of relative weight to the various factors involved in culture and in social organization' (p. 25), or again the search for a hypothetical 'hierarchy' between levels of analysis such as local organization, kinship, collective individuals ('corporate groups'), government and ritual institutions (p. 29). There is no doubt what constitutes the pre-eminent level, even the fundamental variable, for Fortes:

> What is the main methodological contribution of these studies? In my view it is the approach from the angle of political organization to what are traditionally thought of as kinship groups and institutions that has been specially fruitful. By regarding lineages and statuses from the point of view of the total social system and not from that of an hypothetical ego we realize that consanguinity and affinity, real or putative, are not sufficient in themselves to bring about these structural arrangements. We see that descent is a fundamentally *jural* concept as Radcliffe-Brown argued in one of his most important papers (1935); we see its significance, as the connecting link between the external, that is political and legal, aspect of what we have called unilineal descent groups, and the internal and domestic aspect. It is in the latter context that kinship carries maximum weight.... (p. 30, my emphasis) [The 1935 paper referred to is 'Patrilineal and Matrilineal Succession', reprinted in Radcliffe-Brown, *Structure and Function*, RP].

A few comments are necessary to explain the richness of this passage: (1) unilineal descent is not a fact of kinship but a 'politico-jural concept' (let us recall in passing that it was 'succession' that Radcliffe-Brown spoke of in 1935; see above, §12); (2) this concept is more important than that of kinship, because it unites two domains while kinship is confined to just one of them (even if this is the 'source' of the rest, as the continuation of the passage recognises); (3) the total social system leads finally to the politico-jural domain, i.e. to the system of corporate social groups, conceived of as moral persons (as we shall see below). The three propositions we have isolated contain the germ of the whole development of the theory.

Let us start with the third of them: the politico-jural system constitutes the essence of the total social system. All the other institutions appear as a collection of devices whose aim is to ensure the functioning or maintenance of this 'system'. We have seen this for marriage (§12, above). Here even

> [a] society made up of corporate lineages is in danger of splitting into rival lineage factions. How is this counteracted in the interests of wider political unity? (p. 28)

One solution consists in the periodic affirmation of the common interests of the political community, as opposed to the private interests of the component lineages, by institutions and religious sanctions. Moreover, the 'politically integrative functions of ritual institutions' (ibid.) are well known. There is more. All recent studies

> confirm the tremendous importance of the web of kinship as a counterweight to the tendency of unilineal descent grouping to harden social barriers. Or to put it slightly differently, it seems that where the unilineal descent group is rigorously structured within the total social system there we are likely to find kinship used to define and sanction a personal field of social relations for each individual. (pp. 28–29)

Let us note (1) that here is reintroduced the ego who had been sent packing (in fact, a page later, p. 30), and that kinship thus transcends the lineages within which it was intended to confine it; (2) that kinship, or at least its extension, is thus presented as a functional by-product of the lineage system. In short, the fundamental variable – unilineal descent as constitutive of groups seen as moral persons – subordinates both religion and kinship, i.e. the totality of global representations within which the 'system of groups' functions. This reductionism extends to the presentation of an extremely tendentious view of the Yakö system of double unilineal descent: here, precisely where the 'integrative' function is entirely on the matrilineal side, the two unilineal principles are presented as subtly balanced, and we are told of the 'polarity in religious cult and in the political office and authority linked with cult, the legally somewhat weaker matrilineal line being ritually somewhat stronger than the patrilineal line' (p. 34). How can one speak of the relative legal weakness of a group which, in the case of the murder of one of its own members, receives in compensation not only the murderer but also a woman intended to restore the loss suffered? The Yakö case is not one of nuanced equilibrium between two principles of unilineal descent but one in which all the 'integrative functions' of patrilineal groups are on the matrilineal side (as is implicitly recognised on p. 28). This is not how I should like to express these matters, but it is sufficient to oppose to Fortes's atomising and individualist account a reminder of the 'total social system' on which he turns his back in the very act of invoking it. (It would be useful to study and summarise Daryll Forde's article on the Yakö in *African Systems*, bibliog. no. 3, pp. 285ff., in trying to characterise the complementarity between the two modes of unilineal descent. To this end, one might compare David M. Schneider, 'Double Descent on Yap', *Journal of the Polynesian Society*, LXXI/1, March 1962, pp. 1–24.)

We thus notice with Meyer Fortes, compared with Evans-Pritchard, a notable change in the relative positions of the system of unilineal descent groups and the kinship system. This goes along with a notable shift in the conception of unilineal descent groups themselves: while their substantial unity is confirmed, their exogamous character is rendered indistinct. On the first point, it is remarkable that where the emphasis was formerly on segmentation, now it is on 'corporateness', which is to be understood as the unity of the group in itself. The change is a subtle one, and we shall return to it later. As for exogamy, very little is said about it in the 1953 article. The word seems to be mentioned only once, and this in a most remarkable passage. First of all, the general connection between the lineage structure and the ownership of the principal means of production in the society – land, livestock, even artisan monopolies – is stressed. Then we read this:

> A similar connection is found between lineage organization and the control over reproductive resources and relations as is evident from the common occurrence of exogamy as a criterion of lineage differentiation. (p. 35)

It is clear here that, according to this author, exogamy marks the control of reproduction: the very institution which prevents a lineage from reproducing itself by itself is considered in the same way as the possession of lands which allow the descent line [*lignée*] to subsist by itself. This bold generalisation is introduced by means of of the word 'control'. If we were to ask for an explanation, we would probably receive as an answer something like this. In marriage, one of the spouses – the wife in the case of a patrilineage – passes in some degree from one lineage to another. Through payment of a prestation ('bridewealth'), the reproductive powers of the wife are transferred from one lineage to another: there is therefore control. Here is a matter for debate: is it a question of a relationship between lineages, or rather between more restricted groups, or even between relatives who, on one side or the other, are not all members of the same lineage? We would no doubt receive the reply here that all the same it is, broadly speaking, from her lineage that a woman is torn away in order to provide new members for the lineage of her husband. However, it must be very obvious that the prestation signifies at root not control but its opposite, complementarity. I have wished merely to give an example of a mode of thought characteristic of this school, one which we shall find again.

Let us come to Meyer Fortes's real contribution, the introduction, in opposition to 'descent', of 'complementary filiation'. Here, translation into French is especially difficult, since we have only *filiation* for both terms. I propose to use *filiation complémentaire*, it being understood that *unifiliation* is something quite different ('descent'). But what does our author mean by this expression, and what is the utility, the function of this new term for him? We have said that in the English literature the term 'filiation' hardly seems to be used at all. Its first use by Fortes is apparently to be found in the 1953 article which we have been discussing.

> I suppose that we all now take it for granted that filiation – by contrast with descent – is universally bilateral. [...] ... filiation is always complementary [save exceptions, LD] ... (p. 33; cf. *Man*, 1959, no. 331, col. 206a)

It follows that complementary filiation is the chief mechanism producing lineage segmentation and also that it allows degrees of individuation according to the degree to which filiation on the 'non-corporate' side is elaborated (p. 33).

In short, of the two filiations, that with the father and that with the mother, one, being multiplied and going back to an ancestor, serves as the basis for a unilineal descent group or lineage. A very particular attention is given to this privileged line, conceived as jural and political in nature rather than as kinship. But we must recognise that not everything is transmitted through it: membership of a unilineal descent group does not exhaust the totality of relationships, nor even the jural status which attaches to a person or a sibling group. It is everything left over that Fortes includes under the term 'complementary filiation'. One might perhaps expect to find here, following the term literally, a 'complementarity'. In reality, it is the reverse, and the concept is the tool whereby the whole analysis of kinship and the family – domains previously kept apart by Evans-Pritchard – are to be subordinated to unilineal descent. The determination of unilineal descent, be it paternal or maternal, requires complementarily a correlate in the other line by means of which the totality of kinship and the family is reduced to a question of lineality, of the substantial transmission of qualities, whether in full (unilineal descent) or residually (complementary filiation). Thanks to 'complementary filiation', the whole domain is seen as being dominated by groups constituting moral persons, it being understood that this organisation of groups includes certain correlates, which may amount to residual descent.

Naturally, in such a view, every relationship between groups or persons which does not consist either of substantial identity or empirical opposition, of conflict, disappears. It is the same with intermarriage, as we have already seen. Leach has observed that complementary filiation allows relations of affinity to be disguised instead of acknowledged. Here is his judgement on the descent group school, one that is all the more important since the author attaches himself to that school to some extent:

> [The theory] has also served to throw great, and perhaps exaggerated, emphasis upon the principle of descent as the fundamental principle of social organization in all relatively 'homogeneous' societies.

> In all this analysis the stress has been upon ties within the unilinear corporation or between different corporations linked by ties of common descent. The structural ties deriving from marriage between members of different corporations have largely been ignored or else assimilated into the all-important descent concept. Thus Fortes (1953 [bibliog. no. 10]), while recognizing that ties of affinity have comparable importance to ties of descent, disguises the former under his expression 'complementary filiation'. The essence of this concept...is that any Ego is related to the kinsmen of his two parents because he is the descendant of both parents and not because his parents were married. (*Man* 1957, no. 59, col. 54a, bibliog. no. 11, emphasis in the original)

A similar accusation, supported with an African parallel, has been formulated by M.G. Smith: 'It seems likely that the complexity of Fortes' account of Tallensi clanship is due in some part at least to an exclusion of the marriage system from the field of direct analysis' (*Journal of the Royal Anthropological Institute*, LXXXVI/2, 1956, p. 73; see above, §18, note). Fortes replied to Leach's criticism in a long article (*Man*, 1959, nos. 309 and 331, bibliog. no. 11), in which he reaffirms his position with all the clarity one could desire:

> Leach thinks that it is the relationship of marriage and its constituent rela-
> tionships of affinity that form the 'crucial' link between corporate descent
> groups in the Kachin-type system. I would put it the other way round and
> say that marriage and affinity are the *media through which* structurally prior
> politico-jural alliances and associations are expressed and affirmed, and I
> would contend that they are effective as such media because they give rise
> to matrilateral kinship bonds. (209a, emphasis in the original)

In the same article, Fortes refines his definitions of filiation and descent
and provides a fully articulated theory, which only its complexity prevents us from summarising here. Let us simply note that descent is
defined without reference to the corresponding groups (207a) and in
a very general fashion, even though he seems to imply further on that
descent is operative wherever there are such groups, which are by definition 'corporate', even if they possess nothing material (208a). We
shall retain the fact that Fortes's refusal to accord any fundamental
significance to affinity is extended to societies like the Kachin, in
which, as Leach says, such relations are as permanent as the groups
themselves. This lends extra credibility to Smith's criticism.

20. Jack Goody

If there still remained the least doubt as to the profound significance of
Meyer Fortes's terminological refinements and analytical complica-
tions, it would disappear in reading the works of his disciple Jack
Goody, who evinces the same tendencies in an extreme and categorical
form. We shall limit ourselves to an article on the classification of systems of double unilineal descent (*Current Anthropology*, Feb. 1961, pp.
3–25, bibliog. no. 12). Though referring to Rivers, Goody gives
'descent' a wider meaning than that recommended by Rivers or given
by Leach: '"descent" refers to eligibility for membership in kin-groups'
(7b), without excluding cases in which individual choice is possible.
However, he restricts it in practice to cases in which the criterion is
unilineal, since 'this is what is usually meant [by] "double descent"'
(ibid.). In fact, Goody limits his consideration to unilineal descent
groups. The author is even faithful – in part – to the spirit of Rivers
when he writes: 'unilineal descent is...a selection from the totality of
possible kinship ties which serve as a mode of organizing mutually
exclusive groups' (8a).

The question then becomes one of recognising 'groups' founded on
unilineal descent. Among them, Goody accords a pre-eminence to
those which are 'corporate', to those, we would say, which constitute
a moral person; but we shall see that this interpretation is here more

than insufficient, it is totally inaccurate. This difficulty of interpretation is nonetheless a welcome one, for it demonstrates the shift that
Goody inflicts on the notion. The author rejects two of the three crite-
ria retained by Radcliffe-Brown (5a): neither the periodic reuniting of
the members to celebrate a ritual, nor the fact – which Max Weber
retained as essential – of having a representative in the form of a chief
or a council acting on behalf of the entire group finds favour here. To
'avoid confusion', groups with these characteristics are presented as
'assembling or convening groups' and 'pyramidal groups', and the
designation 'corporate' is reserved for those enjoying rights over material objects, '*or, more precisely, within which property is inherited*' (5b). I
have emphasised this particularly arbitrary statement: thus a group
which has a chief and comes together periodically to celebrate a ritual,
which is its property, is not a moral person and lacks the unity of a
constituted body; but it suffices that a group, *without having goods in
common*, is such that individual goods are inherited within it for it to be
considered as having a collective unity. At this point the spirit of Rivers
is totally contradicted, for what he was seeking was precisely to differ-
entiate in vocabulary between the transmission of group membership
and the transmission of goods – individual goods, for example – that he
called inheritance. It is true that Leach has himself written elsewhere:
'Our ultimate concern in all these discussions about the nature of
descent and *filiation* is with the transmission of assets from one generation to another' (*Man*, 1962, col. 131b, bibliog. no. 7, emphasis in the
original), but at least he includes non-material assets, like rights to
names, rituals, etc.

We might wonder at this point whether Goody is truly representative of the profound tendency we have tried to follow from Rivers to
Fortes or whether in reality he represents an exception. We have seen
Fortes ultimately confirm that every unilineal descent group is by definition corporate, adding: 'even if the corporate possession is as imma-
terial as an exclusive common name or an exclusive cult' (*Man*, 1959,
col. 208a, bibliog. no. 11). This passage appears to concern itself with
one consequence of the lack of differentiation of members of the same
lineage, conceived as sharing the same essence, vis-à-vis the outside.
M.G. Smith has very pertinently remarked that, while Evans-Pritchard
only calls a group a 'moral person' (corporation) from empirical observation – goods in common, united action – and refuses this status to
Nuer lineages, as opposed to territorial groups, Meyer Fortes on the
contrary qualifies Tallensi descent lines as 'corporate' simply because
of the dogmatic idea of segmentary opposition between them such as
is revealed by genealogies a priori, as it were (Smith, *Journal of the
Royal Anthropological Institute*, LXXXVI/2, 1956, pp. 58–59). What is
actually at issue here? It is essentially a matter of knowing if social life

is constructed of groups or relations, of knowing whether social anthropology is to be substantialist or structuralist. From this point of view there can naturally be no objection in recognising that groups act conjointly every time they act at all. There is an objection to qualifying as 'moral persons' groups which never act as such, whether the reason for the decision lies in the segmentary form of the genealogies of the lineage or in the a priori idea that the transmission of goods is a social fact of pre-eminent value. From this point of view, Goody and Meyer Fortes represent two stages of the same movement.

It is hardly surprising, therefore, to see Goody recognising as uni-lineal descent groups in the full sense of the term only those within which property is transmitted:

> I therefore suggest the phrase 'double descent' be reserved for full systems
> of the Yakö type in which both descent groups [patrilineal and matrilineal,
> LD] are corporate, that is, in which 'double clanship' is accompanied by
> 'double inheritance'. (bibliog. no. 12, 11a)

In conformity with this definition, Goody does not consider those societies which have, on both the patrilineal and the matrilineal sides, groups characterised and *named* as such as having double unilineal descent. Could anything be more arbitrary? Let us note, furthermore, that the Yakö case, which resists this draconian makeshift, is, as already with Meyer Fortes, interpreted in a very peculiar fashion. Indeed, let us suppose for a moment that movable property is not transmitted in the maternal line among the Yakö: the fact nonetheless remains that it is the matrilineal groups and their priests who are in charge of fertility and peace – their observer, Daryll Forde, has insisted on the central role of such representations in Yakö society. In short, matrilineal groups have charge of life in general and of village unity in particular. But these do not count among the important things for Goody, and, were it not for the transmission of certain goods, he would not recognise matrilineal descent among the Yakö as real at all.

It is not surprising to find that the same author is not interested in exogamy, even though he states the fact in such remarkable terms:

> Other dimensions employed to categorize U[nilineal]D[escent]G[roup]s,
> such as numerical strength and the extent of restrictions upon in-mar-
> riage (exogamy), cannot be discussed here. (5a)

We have reached the summit of reification: the group exists in itself, independently of its relation with other groups; its distinction and dis-creteness no longer depend, as with Rivers, on the clear definition of ties with the outside, and indeed it is not fully real unless tangible realities are transmitted within it. We have here an equivalent of the Hegelian individual, who in order to be real must be reflected in his private property: the 'corporate group' is ultimately, as we have long realised, a collective individual. What is serious is that this collective individual, a facile intermediary between modern mentality and tribal societies, is placed at the head of a hierarchy of concepts that serve to analyse these societies: it is not necessary to go beyond our own concepts in order to understand different societies. In short, scientific research is replaced by a comfortable rationalisation of modern prejudices.

Let us end by pointing out a very useful exercise illustrating the foregoing. It consists in studying three articles on the relationship between the maternal uncle and the uterine nephew in detail and in relation to one another. Radcliffe-Brown's article cited above (bibliog. no. 2) has been criticised by Lévi-Strauss (bibliog. no. 5), and this last in its turn by Goody (bibliog. no. 13; see my note in *Contributions to Indian Sociology*, V, 1961, pp. 77–80). We have here, with regard to a precise problem, a clear idea of the contrast of tendencies involved, and of the difficulties of communication between their representatives.

PART III

THE THEORY OF
MARRIAGE ALLIANCE

G. LÉVI-STRAUSS:
ELEMENTARY STRUCTURES

21. Introduction

The theoretical tendency we shall now examine is very different from
the foregoing. It might be thought more familiar to the French student:
structuralism is in vogue, Lévi-Strauss's thought extends far beyond
the range of his own studies, and his monumental work, *The Elementary Structures of Kinship*, goes back to 1949. But this is perhaps only so
in appearance, especially given the exceptional character of the book.
More personal exploration, not to say exploit, than scientific treatise, it
does not make access to the theory it contains easy, at least as regards
what will be distinguished as the restricted as opposed to the general
theory. A concise summary presenting the essentials of its theory of
cross-cousin marriage in an orderly and rigorous fashion has long been
dreamt of. But it is no longer this that is entirely what is at issue today,
for the work has been taken further in this respect. Here it is proposed
to distil the essence of the restricted theory, which I shall call the theory
of marriage alliance, as brought out in the work of Lévi-Strauss and
that of his continuators. In order to keep things simple, I shall leave
aside the work of his predecessors (but see below, §25).

Elementary Structures is a vast work of extraordinary complexity,
formidable even to the specialist who is relatively familiar with the
topic. Within it, one great idea and an unprecedented sociological
imagination bring together an enormous mass of facts and a collection of varied theoretical problems within a baroque and almost
labyrinthine architecture. On the one hand, there is Australia and the
whole of eastern Asia, from India to the Arctic; on the other, to quote
Edmund Leach, 'at once a contribution to incest theory, a study of the
relevance of reciprocity to all institutionalised forms of marriage, an
analysis of the structural implications of the several varieties of cross-
cousin marriage, and a general theory of social evolution' (*Rethinking
Anthropology*, pp. 76–77). And still the list is not complete. Moreover –
doubtless a function of its very breadth and richness – the work is very

uneven. Adherents of the theory have been irritated by considerable ethnographic mistakes, frequent errors of detail and other sorts of negligence. The specialist who, by degrees, manages more or less to master the work also comes to regret that the author, carried away by his theoretical lyricism, should have juxtaposed, in an extremely discursive presentation, the most definite ideas and important hypotheses with the most tenuous or marginal speculations. There is frequently a discrepancy between the audacity of the constructions and the fragility of their foundations and, more generally, between the work's vast ambitions and its lack of precision and rigour in the tools it uses. The terminology is sometimes less precise than it might be, and, above all, the definitions are generally insufficient, inconsistent, or curiously personal. In what follows, we shall find examples involving concepts which are far from secondary. In short, speculation is given free rein here. The author of these lines must confess that all this has only become fully clear to him after many years: not only has *Elementary Structures* awakened us French from our theoretical slumbers, it has for long fascinated us with the audacity of the perspectives it puts forward and has blinded us to its weaknesses. Apart from its general scientific interest, these weaknesses must be underlined here for two special reasons. On the one hand, they did not go down well with Anglo-Saxon anthropologists used to greater rigour, which has helped increase incomprehension of and hostility towards the theory itself. On the other hand, and above all, the liberties this genius allows himself are deadly to ordinary mortals. We can only admire how he is often able to draw the right conclusions from arbitrary procedures and remedy the errors of the steps he takes through the certainty of his intuition. But this is precisely what cannot be allowed to pass into common usage, and our admiration requires circumspection in ourselves.

Here we must draw from this fresco, conceived as an elaborate philosophical thesis, a commonplace summary, a restricted but, as far as possible, systematic collection of scientific propositions capable of being taught. For this, as when discussing the British school, we shall have recourse to simplification or restriction. And, while committing ourselves, as before, to a careful reading, we shall allow ourselves some liberty as regards the relatively less scientific aspects of the work while drawing support from its successors. Indeed, it has already aged under its own influence, having become the integrating factor of one scientific movement, and the agreement of specialists, in truth few in number, who have accepted and developed the theory allows us to consider the work already from a historical perspective.[7]

---

[7] Unless otherwise stated, all references are to the 1949 French edition, with the corresponding page number for the 1969 English translation added after the slash. The translations of the passages cited are taken from the 1969 translation, except where marked with a row of asterisks, meaning that the passage or other reference in question was omitted from the second French edition of 1967, on which the English translation is based. [This replaces the original note in the French text, RP].

The complexity of *Elementary Structures* is due for one thing to the two theories of kinship, organically linked to each other, that can be distinguished within it: a restricted theory and a general theory.[8] The restricted theory occupies the largest place, and it is that with which we will be concerned. It refers only to societies of a certain type, societies which possess *positive rules* relative to the choice of marriage partner from the point of view of kinship. We should actually say positive rules of a certain type, since these societies uniformly prescribe or prefer marriage between persons falling into the anthropological category of 'cross cousins'. This expression represents an old problem in the discipline, which here receives a rather novel solution. Without being too arbitrary, following Lévi-Strauss and other authors, this restricted theory can be designated the *theory of marriage alliance*. But in *Elementary Structures* it is integrated with a general theory which one can call a structural theory, or, perhaps, to be more precise, a *structuralist theory of kinship*, centred on a structural interpretation of the prohibition of incest.

The incest prohibition is universal. For this reason, instead of trying to explain it, Lévi-Strauss takes it as defining synthetically the essence of kinship: a man cannot marry his close relatives, his sister or his daughter; therefore he must abandon them as wives to other men and receive in return his own wife (or wives) from others. The prohibition of incest is the negative expression of a law of *exchange*, the partial expression of a universal principle of reciprocity, the necessary counterpart to the setting up of social ties between families, from which the constitution of the family itself cannot be separated, as is often done under the influence of common sense. From a sociological point of view the incest prohibition need not be explained: though not a principle of explanation, it is itself a principle of orientation. Indeed, if the parts are explained by the whole, then, for an understanding of the whole of kinship, the incest prohibition must orient us towards societies which possess not only this negative rule, but also positive rules fixing the choice of spouse. Certainly our own societies do not have any, or have lost them. This is, hypothetically, the result of a secondary complication. Luckily, other societies have been preserved in which a simple or elementary structure is attested, one which makes a positive rule correspond directly to a negative rule. These societies conceal the 'explanation' of the incest prohibition under a simple rubric, and a quite particular interest therefore attaches to their study. Such is the link between the general theory and the restricted theory.

---

[8] These expressions have no connection with those of restricted exchange and generalised exchange that will be encountered later on.

Among the main objections to the theory which have been presented, the author had foreseen only one. According to him, men exchange women and not vice versa. This supposes that in all societies it is the men who have the authority, that all societies are 'viripotestal', as it is called, and he adds that this is indeed the case: not even in so-called 'matriarchal' societies, i.e. those very rare ones which have both matrilineal descent and matrilocal residence, can it be claimed that it is the women who exchange the men.

The very idea has scandalised some, in two slightly different ways: on the one hand, women seem to be assimilated to movable goods pure and simple: it is true that the author is sometimes quick to qualify them as the 'most precious good', though elsewhere he takes the opportunity to recall that women figure among the prestations that actually pass from one group to another. Yet we must keep in mind that the woman is not given in the same manner as a slave would be, for example, and that on every occasion one is giving a daughter (or sister) while receiving a wife. In other words, the woman's status is changed by virtue of the prestation. But for those who, like the British, have developed the analysis of the jural aspects of marriage (which rights are transmitted to the husband or his group, and how; which rights the woman retains in her group of origin, etc.), this idea of marriage might seem naive. It is enough to observe that here we have something quite different from what they study, that is – and in particular in the case of the restricted theory – the relationships which accompany marriage for the interested parties, or in other words the forms and implications of what we shall call here 'intermarriage'.

A more radical objection concerns the explanatory value of the notions of 'exchange' and 'reciprocity'. I shall return to this later. It is true that the author can only apply these notions to the modern, individualist view of things by bringing together two agents whose relationship might appear rather arbitrary: the individual subject, e.g. 'I', and opposite him, the agent formed by all the other men in the society under consideration (to the exclusion of certain near relatives). These difficulties can perhaps be avoided by moving away from the letter of *Elementary Structures* to some extent and saying that the incest prohibition bears witness to the fact that an incompatibility, and thus a complementarity, between consanguinity and affinity is always present in some degree, and that societies practising cross-cousin marriage present this opposition in the most logical and complete form. The most marked hostility to Lévi-Strauss's view comes precisely from those who regard consanguinity as an immediate quasi-biological given and not as a notion whose definition depends on that of the notions to which it is related, namely here, the distinctive opposition between consanguinity and affinity. We saw earlier that the English language supports the former interpretation since it promotes the identification of consanguinity with kinship in general, thus imposing the idea, implicit in our own kinship systems, that affinity is external to kinship proper. Certainly from this perspective the incest prohibition is incongruous and seems to call for a psychological explanation.[9]

22. *Elementary Structures*:
General Outline of the Restricted Theory

Throughout the first part of his book, Lévi-Strauss expounds at length on the connection, or passages, from the prohibition of incest to the marriage of cross cousins. Let us try and trace its general development. First of all, the concept of exchange has sometimes been misunderstood. It is a matter of

> the total prestations of which marriage provides both an example and the occasion. ... these total prestations have to do with material goods, social values such as privileges, rights and obligations, and women. The total relationship of exchange which constitutes marriage [is established] between two groups of men, and the woman figures only as one of the objects in the exchange, not as one of the partners between whom the exchange takes place. (p. 148/115)

We see, therefore, that it is in principle not at all a matter of the exchange of a woman *against* other 'objects', but that the exchange of women is a particular aspect of the totality of reciprocal (which does not mean 'identical') prestations between groups. Moreover, each particular marriage is caught within

> a wider cycle of reciprocity, which pledges the union of a man and a woman who is either someone's daughter or sister, by the union of the daughter or sister of that man or another man with the first man in question. (p. 148/116)

It will be noted that the words 'or another man' introduce a considerable extension of the notion of reciprocity, which applies not only if X and Y exchange their sisters in marriage (whether the two prestations

---

[9] A 'refutation' of *Elementary Structures* has been provided by Homans and Schneider (*Marriage, Authority, and Final Causes*, Glencoe, 1955). It concerns mostly the restricted theory and has itself been carefully refuted by Rodney Needham (*Structure and Sentiment*, 1962, bibliog. no. 16). For Homans and Schneider, to base oneself on the interdependence of the features of a kinship system and to consider such a system as a whole logically prior to its parts is to have recourse to an explanation by means of 'final causes', which they exclude.

are made simultaneously or separated by an interval of time), but also if X receives the sister of Y, Y the sister of Z, etc., i.e. in cases where ordinary language would speak rather of 'mutuality' (see below, §32). To return to reciprocity again, and more broadly, it is necessary to quote from a further passage which is obviously important in the mind of the author:

> What are the mental structures to which we have referred and the universality of which we believe can be established? It seems there are three: the exigency of the rule as a rule; the notion of reciprocity regarded as the most immediate form of integrating the opposition between the self and others; and finally, the synthetic character of the gift, i.e., that the agreed transfer of a valuable from one individual to another makes these individuals into partners, and adds a new quality to the valuable transferred. (pp. 108–9/84)

We see from these quotations ('total prestations', 'synthetic character of the gift') that we are moving in the wake of Mauss, as has often been remarked. But let us try and obtain a better idea of how the transition from the prohibition of incest and from 'exchange' in general to the marriage of cousins is effected. The author defines endogamy and exogamy in turn. We know that exogamy is the rule prohibiting marriage within a defined group. Here it is taken to be a 'widened social application of the incest prohibition' (p. 64/51), the sole difference being

> that in exogamy the belief is expressed that the classes must be defined so that a relationship may be established between them, while in the prohibition of incest the relationship alone is sufficient to define ... a complex multiplicity, ceaselessly renewed by terms which are directly or indirectly solidary. (pp. 79–80/62)

An analogous relationship links dual organisation and the marriage of cousins. In dual organisation,

> the members of the community, whether it be a tribe or a village, are divided into two parts which maintain complex relationships varying from open hostility to very close intimacy, and with which various forms of rivalry and co-operation are usually associated. These moieties are often exogamous, that is, the men of one moiety can choose their wives only from the other, and vice versa. (p. 87/69)

There is, then, an obligatory exchange of spouses between the two moieties. Dual organisation is accompanied by a dichotomous division in the kinship terminology: in particular, cousins are classed in two categories. In effect, father's brother's children and mother's sister's children always belong to the same moiety as ego, while father's sister's children and mother's brother's children always belong to the other moiety and are consequently the nearest collaterals (of the same generation) with whom marriage is possible. The former, classed with brothers and sisters, are distinguished by anthropologists as 'parallel cousins'; the latter, designated by terms distinct from those used for the former, are what are called 'cross cousins'. Now marriage between cross cousins is a very widespread institution, one which is not necessarily accompanied by dual organization. Lévi-Strauss observes that it is not necessary, as there was most often a tendency to do in the past, to regard the marriage of cousins as derived from dual organisation. He limits himself to pointing out the 'perfect harmony' that exists between the two, with a characteristic type of kinship terminology (p. 127/99). The relationship is similar to that we have already encountered: just as exogamy establishes, in respect of groups, a prohibition that the incest prohibition is restricted to formulating in individual terms, so dual organisation extends to the whole of society, or to the village, a dichotomy enjoining exchange which the marriage of cross cousins is restricted to constructing around each ego.

> The very nature of the principle of reciprocity allows it to act in two different and complementary ways, either by setting up classes which automatically delimit the group of possible spouses, or by the determination of a relationship, or a group of relationships, so that in each instance it can be said whether a prospective spouse is to be desired or excluded. [...] ... cross-cousin marriage is to be distinguished from the prohibition of incest in that the latter employs a system of negative relationships, and the marriage of cross cousins a system of positive relationships. The incest prohibition says who cannot be married, while the other establishes which spouses are preferred. At the same time, cross-cousin marriage is to be distinguished from dual organization in that the latter has an automatic procedure (unilineal descent) for sorting out individuals into the two categories, while the other has a discriminatory procedure which it applies separately to each individual. (p. 153/119)

The marriage of cousins is therefore a sort of 'turntable' at the 'crossroads of matrimonial institutions', connecting dual organisation with the incest prohibition (p. 156/121). It is also of exceptional interest in that the distinction it establishes between relatives is not at all biological. Morgan and Tylor were wrong in seeking to reduce cousin marriage to other institutions:

What should have been done, on the contrary, was to treat cross-cousin marriage, rules of exogamy, and dual organization as so many examples of one basic structure. This structure should have been interpreted in terms of its total characteristics, instead of being broken up into bits and pieces ... It was especially necessary to see that, of the three types of institution, cross-cousin marriage is the most significant, making the analysis of this form of marriage the veritable *experimentum crucis* in the study of marriage prohibitions. (p. 158/123)

23. Systems with Global Formulas: Australia

The detailed consideration of concrete kinship systems in *Elementary Structures* opens with Australia (pp. 189ff./146ff.). The particular importance of these systems lies in the existence of what I shall call a global formula, which may be that of dual organisation or may be more complicated. From their examination the whole book becomes suffused with the idea that types of cousin marriage correspond to global formulas of exchange. Since this postulate is subject to caution nowadays, I shall take some liberty with our author here. In actually developing the distinction I have just summarised between the individual determination of the spouse and his or her determination by classes or groups, I shall distinguish between the *global* or holistic point of view, in which the entire society appears to be organised into groups linked by a definite formula of intermarriage – as in dual organisation – and what I shall call the individual or *local* point of view, in which rules are referred to a particular ego, as in cross-cousin marriage (as usually formulated). To illustrate the first point of view, I shall take two classic Australian systems, those of the Kariera and Aranda, and present them in a simplified way.[10]

The Kariera tribe had a large number of local groups or 'hordes', all divided into two categories. In this sense we can speak of two 'moieties', moiety membership being transmitted in the paternal line and marriage taking place exclusively between moieties. Thus there would seem to be, at first sight, two patrilineal exogamous moieties. This simple dual image is not entirely accurate, for the 'moieties' whose exis-

---

[10] It so happens that on this particular point Lévi-Strauss accepted the view of these systems that the literature, especially Radcliffe-Brown, provided him with. It now seems possible to simplify their presentation by applying Levi-Strauss's theory precisely to the criticism of previous formulations based on two principles of unilineal descent, one of which is imaginary. See L. Dumont, 'Descent or Intermarriage', *Southwestern Journal of Anthropology*, XXII/3, 1966, pp. 231–50. The article in question is still recent, but it does not seem that the accuracy of the formulas I am going to give in respect of the literature in question – whatever may be the case at the level of the data – need be doubted.

tence we have established are not named as such by the Kariera. In reality, each of the two sorts of local group are divided into two sections, the Kariera tribe thus consisting of four sections in all, and it is these sections that are named, Karimera and Palyeri on one side, Banaka and Burung on the other. The sections of the same local group represent alternating generations: if the father is Karimera, the son is Palyeri and the grandson again Karimera. Intermarriage is not simply between moieties, but between corresponding sections (or generations) of the two moieties. If we designate the two sorts of local group A and B and the two sections within each group 1 and 2, we shall see the generations alternate in the masculine line between A1 and A2 on one side, between B1 and B2 on the other. The masculine members of A1 intermarry with those of B1 and of A2 with B2, it being understood by this that the men of A1 take women from B1 and reciprocally, or if one prefers, that the men of A1 and B1, and of A2 and B2, 'exchange sisters' in marriage in a very general sense. Marriage is usually represented by the sign of equality, and if we insert this sign between square brackets to indicate *inter*marriage (between people of the same sex), we obtain Figure 3a.

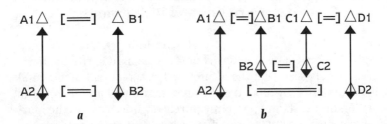

Figure 3.

The Aranda no longer have two but four sorts of local group, and since each local group is divided into two sections, as with the Kariera, this gives eight sections. The formula of intermarriage is that indicated in Figure 3b. The difference from the Kariera case consists in the fact that the two alternating sections of the same local group, e.g. A1 and A2, no longer intermarry with the corresponding sections of the same local group, but with the sections of different local groups: in our diagram, A1 intermarries with B1, but A2 with D2. Reciprocally, it is not difficult to see that if this rule of intermarriage is imposed on a system with the Kariera formula, it will necessarily be transformed into a system with eight sections of the Aranda type. Such is the simplest interpretation that can be placed on these Australian *section systems*,[11] which are, let me repeat, global formulas of the whole society, seen as composed of sections linked together by the alternation of generations in the paternal line on the one hand, and by a very simple law of intermarriage on the other.

As regards the customary interpretation according to which intermarriage, while being recognized, is in practice replaced by the supposition of a mode of descent in the maternal line cross-cutting descent in the paternal line, it can be pointed out that the structural theory allows us to take a much simpler and more logical view. It can be readily understood that the existence of *holistic formulas* of this type does not at all exclude the formulation of the rule of marriage in individual terms in other respects: the Kariera, for example, marry their cross cousins. But the converse is not true, and in general we cannot conclude from marriage between cross cousins to the existence of a holistic formula, whether recognized or not by those involved. This point appears more clearly now than when *Elementary Structures* was published, and it is one to which we shall have to return.

24. Definitions: Restricted Exchange and Generalised Exchange; Harmony and Disharmony

Before passing to the typology of cross-cousin marriage, we should propose definitions of certain terms that will be used in what follows. We have already seen that the idea of *exchange* plays a fundamental role in *Elementary Structures*. It is through this that we are led from the prohibition of incest, an apparently purely negative rule, to the marriage of cousins, the latter form of marriage containing not only the negative rule (the exclusion of parallel cousins) but also its positive counterpart (marriage with cross cousins). One of the author's main preoccupations is to generalise the notion of exchange. What had up to then been called 'exchange' he calls 'restricted exchange'. This is the case in which two men exchange their sisters in marriage, or more generally in which two groups intermarry in both senses, the women born in the one becoming the wives of the men born in the other and

---

[11] I have moved away from the description of the units of the Aranda system as 'subsections'. A brief reflection is enough to show that this description is not a happy one, for it gives precedence to a substantialist and pseudo-historical approach (in which the Kariera section is divided into two Aranda subsections, whereas it is the number of local groups that are distinguished which is multiplied by two) over a structuralist one: in the latter, in both cases the section is the same sort of subdivision of the local group and of the unit of global intermarriage.

vice versa, as in the Kariera example, between the respective sections of the two sorts of local group A and B. More generally:

> The term 'restricted exchange' includes any system which effectively or functionally divides the group into a certain number of pairs of exchange-units so that, for any one pair X–Y there is a reciprocal exchange relationship. (p. 189/146)

What, now, is 'generalised exchange'? It is, in fact, a system in which, between two defined 'partners', exchange is no longer reciprocal, but unilateral or oriented: if P gives (wives) to Q, then Q in his turn gives to another partner R (and not to P in return), and thus R to S, etc. In order for the system to be viable, it is obviously necessary for the chain to be closed, i.e. the first giver in the chain, P, receives wives from another partner, let us say Z. This is what Dutch authors working on Indonesia called 'circulating connubium', e.g. from P to Q, from Q to R, etc., from Y to Z and *from* Z to P. In fact, the author did not bring the *unilaterality* of the 'exchange' to the fore right at the outset, speaking rather of 'indirect' exchange, for example (p. 271/215–16, but cf. pp. 229 30/ 177–78, etc.). We shall see in what follows that, while restricted exchange corresponds to marriage between the bilateral cross cousins, generalised exchange corresponds exclusively to marriage with the matrilateral cross cousin (mother's brother's daughter). But what particularly interests our author is the difference in the integrative capacity of the two systems: while the first can never *unite* more than one pair of 'exchange partners', only *juxtapose* them, the second can ideally unite any number of partners from three upwards.

In conformity with his general point of view, Lévi-Strauss has sought to characterise kinship systems, not, as with other authors, from a feature or 'variable' which is considered to be primordial, but from a global point of view (relations of exchange between units) and also from the point of view of the system of features that characterises them. Among the institutions or abstract features which may characterise a kinship system, there is certainly the positive marriage rule for those systems that possess them – the only ones, let us remember, which interest us here. But there is also descent, residence, etc., and all these features must be interrelated: particular descent rules, residence rules and marriage rules cannot be combined indifferently.

The general hypothesis is a relatively refined one. There is sometimes a tendency to presuppose a simple relationship between descent and marriage rule, perhaps, for example, that the preference for one or other of the two cross cousins, patrilateral or matrilateral, may be linked respectively with matrilineal or patrilineal descent. Lévi-Strauss's hypothesis is, at first sight, more complex. He distinguishes two cases: descent and residence are either in the same line (whether paternal or maternal), in which case one says that the system is 'harmonic' (p. 270/214–15) and a rule of matrilateral marriage (generalised exchange) is to be expected, for reasons which will appear more clearly in what follows; or else descent and residence are in two different lines, paternal *and* maternal, in which case one says that the system is 'disharmonic' (ibid.) and one would expect a rule of bilateral marriage (or restricted exchange). The degree of probability of these hypotheses inevitably escapes us at the moment, so let us content ourselves with retaining the principle, namely the attempt to form the main abstract features of kinship into a true system, an attempt which is without precedent.

To be candid, things look rather different when one searches the book for a precise definition of the features or variables in question. As regards descent, to begin with, the general orientation of the work – the emphasis placed on marriage and exogamy – would seem to indicate that, explicitly or implicitly, the definition must be that of Rivers, which we have referred to above as unilineal descent. And in fact this is certainly what is involved in *Elementary Structures* wherever descent is mentioned, i.e. the unilineal transmission of the membership of an exogamous group (see, for example, middle of p. 126/98). It is true that this is quite different from what we are told in a long passage treating descent quite systematically (pp. 133–36/103–7). Here, the word is taken in a very vague or rather a variety of senses, including an extremely broad one ('a social kinship link between a child [and one of its parents, LD]': p. 133/103) and a more exact one which is familiar to us from English usage: 'the transmission of...rights and...obligations' – of name, social status, goods and prerogatives (p. 135/105). Thus the author distinguishes unilateral descent, cognatic descent and finally bilateral descent for the case of the 'juxtaposition of two unilineal rules of descent, each governing exclusively the transmission of certain rights' (p. 135/106). But in the discussion which immediately follows this (pp. 136ff./106ff.) he immediately slides, under the same term 'bilaterality',[12] into examples of exogamy in both lines, i.e. what we have called, following Rivers, double unilineal descent (Ashanti, Toda, Yakö). Here, in my view, is the true working concept of 'descent' in this work, and it is obvious that if one wanted to broaden it, as the author seems to do on the pages cited, it would render the definitions of harmony and disharmony more uncertain.

---

[12] Following criticism, Lévi-Strauss made his terminology more precise in the 1967 edition: on the corresponding pages, descent is now said to be 'lineal', the 'laterality' thus being reserved for marriage. [The page numbers cited in the French original prove to be wrong and have thus been omitted here as uncertain, RP].

As regards residence now, this is generally called patrilocal or matrilocal according to whether local groups are perpetuated in the paternal or maternal line. In simple terms, this supposes that it is the woman who goes at marriage to live with her husband (one thus says 'virilocal' residence) or conversely the husband who goes to live with his wife (called 'uxorilocal' residence). (The matter is in reality more complicated in the literature, for under the same term 'residence' other perspectives may be substituted for that with which we are concerned here.) It certainly seems that in *Elementary Structures* residence often assumes the meaning just given. However, if we refer to a passage already cited (p. 270/214), in which the author defines what he means by harmony and its opposite, we find something a little different. In fact, the representative of disharmony here is the Kariera system, 'with its matrilineal moieties and two patrilocal groups' (p. 271/215, cf. p. 208/160–61). This may strike the reader as strange, for, in our presentation of the Kariera section system, we made short work of the *supposed* matrilineal descent of this group and replaced it with the full recognition of the effects of intermarriage between sections. Whatever the facts of the matter, what should concern us here is another aspect of our author's formula: what he regards as 'residence' among the Kariera has more than its usual meaning, for it is nothing less than the transmission of membership in an exogamous group *which is at the same time a local group*, i.e. descent in the full sense of the term, endowed into the bargain with a local aspect, as it were. In fact, in the mind of the author, disharmony results here from a double mode of descent, or, if one will, from exogamy in both lines, paternal and maternal, and the local or residential aspect is supplementary to it. In other passages, on the other hand, residence often assumes its usual meaning when, for example, the two types of harmonic regime, patrilineal and patrilocal, matrilineal and matrilocal, are named (p. 270/214–15); or again, in the passage emphasising the rarity of regimes that are matrilineal and matrilocal (the Nayar, etc.) and the tension which, according to the author, characterises regimes that are matrilineal and patrilocal (pp. 149–52/116–18). In short, in conformity with the author's idea, we can be sure that there will be disharmony whenever there is double unilineal descent (with residence in one line in the simpler cases), but we can be less sure that there will really be disharmony between descent on the one hand and residence pure and simple on the other if they are in opposite lines.[13]

---

[13] As I myself supposed in an application of the theory which is already quite old: *Hierarchy and Marriage Alliance*, p. 20 (bibliog. no. 19).

25. Cross-Cousin Marriage: Bilateral Form

Here we come to the heart of the matter. I now propose to collect together for convenience the characteristics of the three forms of intermarriage which correspond respectively to marriage with the bilateral cross cousin, the matrilateral cross cousin and the patrilateral cross cousin. We shall certainly be following *Elementary Structures* quite closely, but we must not forget on the one hand that these forms had already been isolated earlier, and on the other that Lévi-Strauss does not characterise them at all systematically, but only discursively, in the course of his account. We shall take advantage of this in order to assume the freedom of viewing them as they appear to us today, i.e. of exploiting this opportunity for subsequent reflection. In particular, a distinction, as far as possible, between the *local* and *global* aspects of the implications involved (see above, §23) seems indispensable. (For a bibliographic supplement to *Elementary Structures* and a history of the treatment of the second form of marriage, see Leach, *Rethinking Anthropology*, pp. 64ff. and p. 55; for the three types, ibid., p. 59; they had already been clearly characterised in an old note by Fortune not mentioned by Lévi-Strauss: R.F. Fortune, 'A Note on Some Forms of Kinship Structure', *Oceania*, IV, 1933, 1–9.)

In order to study the properties of these theoretical types, it is convenient to plot them with diagrams. It is merely necessary to give a precise meaning to each element of the diagram and to take care when passing from the diagram to reality. The symbols used in *Elementary Structures* have been adopted generally here: men are represented by triangles, women by circles, marriage by the sign =, siblingship by a horizontal line; generations succeed from top to bottom, filiation between parents and children is marked by a vertical line (or oblique line, according to the requirements of the figure) issuing from a marriage sign.

The bilateral type corresponds to the exchange of sisters renewed from generation to generation. It is enough merely to plot this type of intermarriage to see immediately that, in each marriage, the spouses are double cross cousins: a man always marries a woman who is simultaneously the daughter of his mother's brother and of his father's sister. In order to make clear all the properties involved, let us suppose a double mode of unilineal descent, patrilineal (X and Y) and matrilineal (A and B). Let us choose to emphasise patrilineal descent in plotting vertically the relationship between the men of the two lines X and Y respectively. Matrilineal descent affects the descendants as indicated in Fig. 4. We can readily establish the following:

(1) From the *local* point of view, the permanence of the patrilineal character of the male line is accompanied by the general alternation, for a given horizontal position, of the matrilineal characters A and B: each of these characters is reproduced in the same position two generations below; generation 3 reproduces generation 1 exactly, generation 4 reproduces generation 2. Finally, it is easy to ascertain that every individual marries a person who is doubly related to him or her as a cross cousin on the paternal and maternal sides simultaneously. Let us take, for example, the man X of generation 2 (the solid triangle) who is of matriline B. His wife is simultaneously the daughter of his paternal aunt and his maternal uncle – she is his bilateral cross cousin.

(2) From the *global* point of view, there is reciprocal and total exchange between lines X and Y, intermarriage in two senses, very obviously *restricted exchange* in our definition of the term. Moreover, we see that our hypothesis of double unilineal descent and thus of disharmony accords perfectly with this form of intermarriage, which ensures the reproduction of the same characters in alternating generations: 1 and 3, 2 and 4.

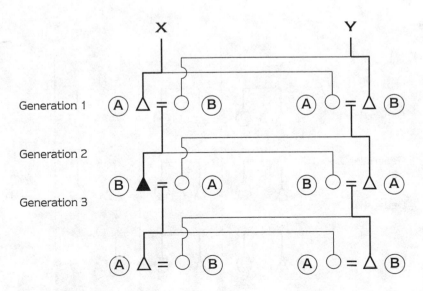

Figure 4. Cross-cousin Marriage: Bilateral Form

26. Cross-Cousin Marriage: Matrilateral Form

In this type of intermarriage, a man marries exclusively his matrilateral cousin, the daughter of his maternal uncle. In order to represent this it is convenient, as before, to plot a brother and a sister in each generation and in each line, but the formula demands at least three brother–sister pairs in each generation. To obtain a schematic representation of this type of intermarriage, it is sufficient to plot a chain of at least three pairs linked by marriage as below (Fig. 5) and to repeat it exactly in the following generations. We shall link the successive generations with oblique lines of descent. A line sloping to the right of our figure and in the direction of a brother–sister pair will appropriately indicate patrilineal descent, the son appearing exactly beneath his father. (If we were to incline the descent line in the opposite direction, the uterine nephew would appear below the maternal uncle, an appropriate representation of matrilineal descent.)

Let us call the three patrilines X, Y and Z. We shall leave the chain open at the two extremes, without prejudice to the number of 'exchange' units in the system, and shall consider a man, ego, situated in the middle line, Y. The following properties will be noted (Fig. 5):

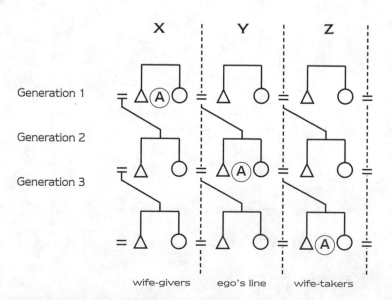

Figure 5. Cross-cousin Marriage: Matrilateral Form

1. From the *local* point of view:
a) The model is oriented. The marriage of a man and that of his sister differ in the sense that, while ego marries into X, his sister marries into Z. At the same time, the marriage of any man is in this case similar to that of his father (or of his maternal uncle with matrilineal descent): all the men of succeeding generations in Y marry into X; similarly, all the women born into Y marry into Z, the marriage of every woman being in this case similar to that of her paternal aunt (or of her mother with matrilineal descent).
b) From the points of view of patrilineal descent and of marriage, successive generations reproduce themselves exactly.
c) For line Y, lines X and Z have a fixed role: X are wife-givers, Z are wife-takers; line Y is itself wife-taker to X, wife-giver to Z. Although at least three units are necessary (with only two units, one would fall back into the bilateral formula), the orientation of the relation of intermarriage is expressed very satisfactorily as a simple opposition between givers and takers (the *mayu/dama* of the Kachin).
d) In contrast to the bilateral form, we see that in this case a given line does not depend exclusively on any other single line for all the marriages of its members, and simultaneously that successive generations do not in any way differ among themselves. Two conditions in this case bring out the 'exchange' unit more clearly within the network of relationships, solidifying it, as it were. This is true in the plan of the kinship terminology, and also, as Lévi-Strauss strongly insists, in that of the relative hierarchical status of the units. A status difference will probably be established between 'givers' and 'takers', the question of which is superior, which inferior, being reserved for the moment. Let us merely retain here the idea that this form of intermarriage 'presupposes equality, and is a source of inequality' (p. 325/266).
2. From the *global* point of view:
a) We have recognised in this form of oriented intermarriage – which is no longer reciprocal between two given units – the formula of *generalised exchange* defined above. Instead of being limited to only two units, this form can unite any number of units, odd or even, from three upwards. It has greater possibilities in integrating several units into a single system. And, adds our author, it allows and promotes diversity (p. 353/288–89).
b) Correlatively, this form presents problems in its functioning: in order to function the chain must be closed; the first unit, that which gives in order to start the chain off, must ultimately receive in return from the last; ideally the global system is represented by a circle. The return of the initial gift is 'postponed'; consequently, so that the gift may be agreed to, there has to be some certainty

about the return: there is an element of 'speculation'. And yet does the circle really close? This is not at all certain if it is a long circle and if a difference of status is regularly established between units, as has been supposed, for at the point of supposed closure there would ultimately be a considerable difference of status, and in a direction opposed to what is recognised in the remainder of the chain. We shall return to this point later. Let us merely observe here that, just as the local features correspond to observation, so the global features are hypothetical, for once again we have no guarantee that a global model really exists in fact or that it effectively results from the individual determination of the marriage with which it is concerned.

c) It will have been noticed that, in contrast to the preceding form, I have introduced only a single mode of descent in this form. Indeed, according to our author, the form corresponds to a harmonic system, in which everything is transmitted in the same line. What would happen if we introduced a disharmony? Let us suppose that the first generation of X has an attribute A which is transmitted in the maternal line. It can readily be seen that it would be transmitted from X1 to Y2 and from Y2 to Z3. If the system only consists of the three units X, Y and Z, there would be intermarriage between X and Z and the attribute A would pass in consequence from Z3 to X4. More generally, if n is the number of units in the system, the attribute transmitted in the maternal line will reappear in the patriline in generation $(n + 1)$; it is absent throughout the interval, with this difference from what happened in the bilateral case: there is no alternation of generations, and the attribute transmitted in the maternal line has no relevance for the generations immediately following X1. It is probably this feature which, joined to the study of concrete systems of pure matrilateral type, led Lévi-Strauss to conclude that disharmony was impossible in this case. The discussion is difficult and doubtless not very fruitful at the present level. It must be realised that the matrilateral form as put forward in *Elementary Structures* represents an ideal form, coherent, clearly opposed to the bilateral form, though it corresponds well to certain concrete systems that have been described (Kachin, Gilyak). But if we take the term 'disharmony' in its textual sense of a contrast between descent and residence, and if we take 'residence' in its usual sense, in which exogamy is not involved, we can then imagine the matrilateral form functioning in a disharmonic system with, for example, patrilineal descent and matrilocal residence. Let us distribute at random a certain number of residences *a, b, c, d*, etc. on our diagram between the different units without feeling obliged to give a different residence to two successive units

in the chain. All that can be said is that in such a system the patrilines will be dispersed among different localities and that the link
between the different features of the system will be less strict than
it would otherwise be, residence not being organically linked to the
other two features. For all that, is it in fact impossible? This is something that only direct observation can decide.

27. Cross-Cousin Marriage: Patrilateral Form

In this form, a man marries exclusively the daughter of his paternal
aunt. It can be plotted and its theoretical properties listed, but of all the
three forms it is the least attested, yet the most discussed in both *Elementary Structures* and its successors.

In order to represent it conveniently (Fig. 6), we can draw in
brother–sister pairs underneath one another as with the matrilateral
form, but care must be taken to reverse the direction from one generation to another. Let there be three patrilines, X, Y and Z. (It will be seen
that, in order to have a vertical succession of 'pairs', it is necessary to
incline the lines of descent alternately towards the left and the right.)
The following remarks can be made:

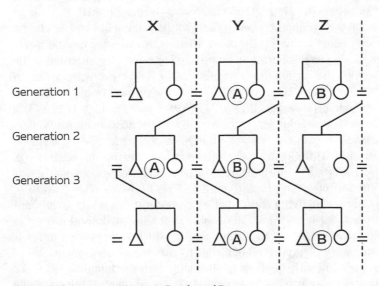

Figure 6. Cross-cousin Marriage: Patrilateral Form

Locally:

a) As with the matrilateral form, the marriage of a man is different from that of his sister, while his daughter and then his grandson marry in the same line as himself: generation 3 reproduces generation 1, even from the point of view of the second mode of descent, which would be matrilineal (A, B) in our figure. There is therefore alternation of generations as in the bilateral form.

b) As the reversed arrangement of pairs which we have had recourse to shows, there is an inversion of marriages between two successive generations: in Y1 the brother marries into Z, the sister into X, but it is the opposite in Y2. Thus at least three units are necessary here too. In any given generation, the chain of intermarriages is similar to that in the matrilateral form; the difference consists in the fact that in this case the orientation is reversed in each generation: in generation 1 women pass from Z towards Y towards X, in generation 2 from X towards Y towards Z. This thus approaches the bilateral formula. We might almost say that there is restricted exchange between, for example, Y and Z, but with return deferred: it is in generation 2 that Y returns, as it were, to Z the woman which it has received in generation 1. But it is not really restricted exchange, for it is not exclusive: in the same period Y has given to, and then received from X.

Globally:

Many comparative remarks could be made here. The essential thing is the combination of characteristics, some of which recall the bilateral system, others the matrilateral system. On the one hand, there is direct or reciprocal exchange between two groups, but partial and extending over two generations; on the other, there is the oriented circulation of women in a given generation, but instead of remaining oriented in the same way, this circulation reverses itself every other generation. In reality, our author is not very clear as to the properties of this form of intermarriage (see especially pp. 250/199ff. and pp. 530–1/426–28). He denies the circular aspect to some extent because he unduly generalises the aspect of reciprocal exchange. At the same time, he seems to think that this form corresponds to a harmonic regime (p. 274/217–18) (like the matrilateral form) and to recognise that there is alternation of generations (pp. 142, 254/110–11, 202–4 and Ch. XIII). These somewhat contradictory considerations relate to different examples, but it is equally noticeable that the patrilateral form was incidentally forced on an author whose effort was oriented towards the necessity of giving recognition to the matrilateral form and of characterising it through its relationship with the bilateral form. We shall see later that serious doubts have been raised as to the existence of the form in reality. It is not to be doubted, however, that the subjects themselves are often perfectly conscious of the properties of this model, for example, in south India. Moreover, such is the case in general for the three forms, and were this not so the theoretical models would have little interest. At the same time, however, one suspects that the reality of intermarriage does not directly produce any of these models. It is in the relationship between reality and model that all the difficulty lies. To give only one example, it is one of the general conclusions of the long study of matrilateral marriage to which Lévi-Strauss devotes himself that generalised exchange will never be free from a certain foreign element, which the author ultimately identifies not with restricted exchange, but with patrilateral marriage, which – more or less allied with 'avuncular privilege', i.e. the case in which the maternal uncle can reclaim his sister's daughter for himself – haunts the opposite orientation like a ghost (pp. 483–85, 564/389–92, 453–54).

It is also, to a great extent, around the question of the relationship of reality to the theoretical model that the discussions and modifications which have followed the publication of *Elementary Structures* have been situated, and which I shall return to later. Perhaps I have anticipated certain points a little in the interests of clarity. In particular, I might have remarked that, in departing from an *individual rule of marriage* (supposedly obligatory) with a particular cousin, what we have sought to characterise are *the forms or types of intermarriage between theoretical elementary units*. Certainly this was so at the time of *Elementary Structures*, but the fact appears more clearly today. A great many of the difficulties that the study has encountered and of the discussions it has given rise to are due to the formulation of the type of intermarriage in the language of 'individual' relations of kinship (certainly *individual*, in so far as they are always centred on an individual ego, but also *classificatory* in their definition) and to the formulation of these relationships themselves in the anthropological language of 'cross cousins'. All this will be clarified a little more in what follows. For a recent statement, see David Maybury-Lewis, 'Prescriptive Marriage Systems' (bibliog. no. 17).

28. Cross-Cousin Marriage and Kinship Terminology

The consideration of kinship terminologies has a large place in *Elementary Structures*. This is justified in principle not only by their intrinsic interest, but also from a practical point of view. Indeed, the author undertook an extended comparative study from a body of ethnographic literature which varied greatly in age and quality, but in which

the kinship terminology had generally been collected and often constituted the most complete and definitive document relating to kinship. Let us recall that the analysis and even the recording of these
terminologies suffered discredit in recent British anthropology attributable in part to the 'pseudo-historical' interpretations of earlier
authors. Rivers in particular had striven too hard to explain the pecu-
liarities of the terminologies as survivals of *supposed* earlier forms of
marriage. But there is something more solid involved here. Certainly
Lévi-Strauss does not always deny himself more or less speculative historical reflections, but with the aid where necessary of its successors,
one can extract from *Elementary Structures* a general idea of the synchronic relationship between kinship terminology (in its pattern
and/or certain of its features) and the different forms of cousin marriage. This is briefly what I shall do here.

The general and characteristic feature of the terminologies which
corresponds to cross-cousin marriage is the absence of distinct terms
for affinal relatives. There may be words for 'wife' and 'husband', but a
man will designate his father-in-law, for example, by the same term
that he uses for his maternal uncle. This has been known for a long
time. For the rest, we must distinguish from the outset two types of
vocabulary, one symmetric, the other asymmetric. The symmetric type
is the most familiar: it corresponds, *Elementary Structures* insists, just
as much to dual organisation as to the bilateral form of cross-cousin
marriage or 'restricted exchange'. One can add here the patrilateral
form of cross-cousin marriage. The asymmetric type, very different
from the preceding, has much less clear contours. It corresponds to the
matrilateral form of cross-cousin marriage or 'generalised exchange'.

What I have just designated as the symmetric type is what the literature calls the 'bifurcate merging' type; *for a given generation and sex, all
relatives are divided into two categories and two only*, at least in the medial
generations. We have already encountered this characteristic in ego's
generation in distinguishing between parallel and cross (cousins), it
being understood that the parallel category contains not only those we
call cousins but also actual brothers and sisters. It is an easy matter to
extend this distinction to the adjacent generations. In the father's generation the father himself, the father's brother and also the mother's
sister's husband all fall into one category, which we can call 'parallel',
while the mother's brother and father's sister's husband fall in the
opposite, or 'cross', category. Similarly, the mother's sister will be a
'parallel' relative, the father's sister a 'cross' relative. These expressions
explain nothing, and merely describe the general division of relatives
into two categories.

This arrangement supposes that the generations (and relative–age
groups, elder–younger), as well as the two sexes, are rigorously distin-

guished. Two successive generations are never brought together or identified; if this happens, it is between generations separated by an intermediate generation (grandfather and grandson). This tendency to alternate the generations should not be surprising in view of the diagrams of the corresponding forms of marriage (above, §§25, 27).[14]

The asymmetric type differs from the preceding one in two ways: on the one hand, the two sorts of cross cousin, and cross kin generally on the 'maternal' and 'paternal' sides, are kept apart, this corresponding to the unilaterality of intermarriage and the distinction between wife-givers and wife-takers; on the other hand, there is a tendency to confuse generations by grouping into the same category relatives belonging to different generations, on the one hand among the wife-givers, on the other among the wife-takers. We have seen how, with matrilateral marriage (above, §26), successive generations of allies of a particular sort appear to be identical (in a harmonic regime), the line in question tending to present itself as a bloc. In the terminology, for example, the wife-givers may be assimilated to the fathers-in-law and the wife-takers to the sons-in-law, which suggests a hierarchical relationship, the former being superior, the latter inferior. One cannot, of course, interpret this as depending simply on the unity of the lineage, for the fact is that when the lineage is treated thus it is being seen from the outside, in a unilateral relationship of affinity and with the corresponding hierarchical status.

I have spoken of a 'tendency', and I warned earlier that this type is not bounded as strictly as the preceding one. In order to account for the variability found within the type it is sufficient to compare, in *Elementary Structures*, the Gilyak terminology (Fig. 55/54, p. 365/297) and that of the Kachin. In the latter case, the assimilation of generations is still not very clear in the 1949 edition (p. 295) and the author does not dwell upon it; it appears more clearly in the 1967 edition (p. 273 and p. 280/pp. 235ff.).[15]

Here, approximately, is what can be said about these phenomena in general. *Elementary Structures* contains neither a systematic theory nor a systematic methodology. We can only state how the author proceeds with regard to each case (from a different point of view, moreover, from that which has been retained here). Among other things,

---

[14] There are notable differences, still ill-explored, within this type, for example, between the systems called Iroquois, Dravidian and Australian. Thus Radcliffe-Brown still spoke of the 'Australo-Dravidian' system, although an important difference distinguishes the two, which seems to correspond well to that between the presence or absence of a global system of intermarriage (see my article on the Kariera vocabulary in J. Pouillon and P. Maranda, eds, *Échanges et Communications, Mélanges offerts à Claude Lévi-Strauss*, Paris and The Hague: Mouton, 1970, pp. 272–86). [Reprinted as 'The Kariera Kinship Vocabulary: An Analysis', in L. Dumont, Affinity as a Value, Chicago: University of Chicago Press, 1983, Ch. 5, RP].

[15] At lines 11–12, p. 280 (1967edn.)/lines 8, 10, p. 242, we should obviously read: *dama* of *dama*; *mayu* of *mayu*.

we read on p. 155/120-21 that the assimilation of cross relatives in the father's generation to the relatives of the spouse is an indication of the marriage of cousins; the most systematic examples are perhaps those on pp. 295/***, 335/274–75, 339/277–79 and 364/296ff. (the latter a very full account of matrilateral marriage among the Gilyak). Here is the passage relating to the Kachin:

> There can be no doubt as to the interpretation of the [terminological, LD] system. The dichotomy of cousins, uncles and aunts into cross and parallel; identification of the mother's brother with the wife's father; of the niece and nephew as children-in-law; of the father's sister with the husband's mother; the absence of any terms for spouse...everything suggests a system of marriage between cross cousins and, more particularly (since the terms for parents-in-law differ for a man and a woman) between sister's son and brother's daughter [i.e. matrilateral, LD]. (p. 296/***)

Can we go no further in the structural analysis of the terminologies? Let us say quite clearly that there is something unsatisfactory in the study of the terminologies in *Elementary Structures*. There are several reasons for this. First, there is the enormous quantity of material which is dealt with, often reproduced in detail and even in a table, compared with the considerable and sometimes fruitless amount of time that would be needed to clarify just one of these terminologies only a little. Then we know, from an article published a few years before the book, that the author did not at that time believe in a rigorously structured analysis of the terminology in isolation [cf. Editor's Introduction, note 5, RP]. This no doubt explains the fact that he was content on the one hand to reproduce the data, on the other to extract from it, as with the Kachin, whatever appeared useful to him in *bringing them into an immediate relationship* with the other aspects of the kinship system. However, the author realised which method to follow, witness this passage from page 331/***, where he envisages

> a schematic representation which satisfies the sole condition that the greatest possible number of the meanings of each term correspond to the smallest possible number of positions in the structure. The ideal – rarely realized for all terms – is that all the meanings of a given term correspond to one position, and to one only.

The principle he proposes is unfortunately scarcely applied. Justifying himself by virtue of the profound changes which certain systems are supposed to have undergone and the practical difficulties involved, the author introduces in the same passage what he calls, rather curiously, a 'reduced model', in which, according to him, only the central area functions correctly, the marginal areas being in shadow. I confess I have never completely understood these 'reduced models'. If they are unsatisfactory, it is because the author actually restricts himself to marking the term corresponding to each relative on a grid representing a definite type of marriage, which most of the time is of the matrilateral type: the terminology is never considered in itself according to a scheme which fulfils the requirements indicated in the passage quoted; on the contrary, it is at the outset referred to a theoretical marriage scheme, laid on the Procustean bed, so to speak, of a fixed and unvarying grid pattern. Nowhere does this methodological insensitivity appear more clearly than in respect of the Maria Gond, a tribe of south India. Whereas the literature that is summarised on pp. 487–88/393–95 clearly indicates patrilateral marriage, the author chooses to plot it as matrilateral, with this bizarre and astonishing result: Figure 76/75 itself very summarily provides a matrilateral grid, on which the sole obvious feature is the alternation of generations, a feature which is obviously patrilateral.

29. Conclusion: The Contribution of *Elementary Structures*

The foregoing calls for all sorts of additional comments. Let me recall that I merely wished to introduce briefly and, I hope, in scientific form the fundamental concepts of Lévi-Strauss's restricted theory, in short, that is to say, the theory of kinship systems which have not only negative but also positive rules relating to marriage, i.e. classificatory or individual rules which might approximate in this second language to the general term of cross-cousin marriage. Not only have I had to leave aside the whole of the rich presentation of concrete systems that swells this vast book – and with it the historico-cultural preoccupations with the history of these systems and their reciprocal contacts and influences that appear from time to time – but I have also had to sacrifice the greater part of the superabundant production of ideas that the author's sociological imagination lavishes on its whole length. Nor have I been able to give any idea of the extraordinary ingenuity which he deploys in the analysis of the data and the discovery or invention of relationships between them. To tell the truth, we might even wonder whether he has not in the end tried to draw too much from a very variable and unequal body of material. Has he not, as the opponents of his theory never miss an opportunity to accuse him – and a little like Rivers before him – viewed marriage as the deus ex machina of kinship and the efficient cause of all sorts of other phenomena? Thus he traces the elder–younger distinction, which is so widespread, to a particular characteristic of marriage, as in the following passage relating to the Wikmunkan of Australia:

> The subdivision of each generation into two age classes, 'older' and 'younger', is thus in direct correlation with the possibility of two men vying for the one woman. [...] ... this dichotomy of generations always appears in such circumstances, and ... it must be seen as a normal function of systems of alternate marriage. (p. 263/209)

Even if this is often the case, in this form the generalisation seems to take little notice of a fundamental sociological tendency: *hierarchy* is expressed here in the form of a hierarchical distinction between elder and younger. Is there not here a tendency which is infinitely more widespread than optional marriage and is consequently endowed with a greater explanatory value?

The most important criticisms that can be made are those constructive ones which have in fact been made by adherents of the theory subsequently, and to some extent by the author himself, and I shall deal with these shortly. Just a couple of words are needed here to determine ideas on certain points to which we shall not have occasion to return. I have noted the difficulties surrounding the notions of harmony and disharmony. There is indisputably a relationship between disharmony and the symmetric formula on the one hand, and between harmony and the matrilateral formula on the other. But these relationships correspond to the maximum coherence between the different features: nowhere is it said that a concrete system cannot exist with a lesser degree of coherence than the maximum. Examining this is a matter of empirical investigation and, besides, the author himself does not make the mistake of emphasising the mixing of the two formulas or tendencies.

Having confined myself, as I said at the start, to the restricted theory or theory of marriage alliance, we have said nothing concerning what our author calls 'complex structures' as opposed to 'elementary structures'. It is precisely these which correspond to the absence of any positive marriage rule, i.e. cases in which the determination of the spouse does not result from kinship alone (p. ix/xxiii). The idea that these structures result from the development or combination of elementary structures appears only rarely (p. 574/463–64). In fact, what falls into the 'complex' class is everything that is not 'elementary', amongst other things, kinship among ourselves, Crow-Omaha systems, and those systems called cognatic (passage added to the 1967 edition, p. 124/translation pp. 104–5).

To me, it seems that anthropology realises more and more clearly the difficulties involved in passing from semi-abstract theories, corresponding often to particular regional cultures, to a universal theory which encompasses them. The quite strict relationship that exists between the theory of unilineal descent groups and African societies, or at the very least certain ones, has been appreciated. In the same fashion, the theory of marriage alliance is undoubtedly indispensable for the societies of Southeast Asia. On the other hand, it is inapplicable to Arab societies practising patrilateral [*patrilinéaire* in the original, RP] parallel-cousin marriage. Both theories are disarmed in the face of those systems known as cognatic or undifferentiated where one might say, paraphrasing Lévi-Strauss himself, that kinship does not allow itself to be separated from the relationship with the soil and where one sees that, to isolate a true 'system', it is necessary to reunite them. In short, we are still, as is said, 'at a low level of abstraction', and the most interesting theories we have at our disposal are each applied to just one type of society or one type of system in particular. This state of things poses vast and difficult tasks for us, but there is no reason for complaint here, for it is the price to be paid for the global grasp of the social that is anthropology's lot and anthropology's alone.

Whatever reservations one might have about particular developments or aspects of *Elementary Structures,* it must never be forgotten, first of all that, as we said at the start, we sometimes find profound ideas concluding debatable presentations. But above all, the value of the book results from the contrast, which should be clear from our account, between its fundamental inspiration and the inspiration which underpins the development of British anthropology, notwithstanding one glorious exception. Lévi-Strauss has not only drawn attention to important aspects of social life that British anthropology increasingly lost sight of after Rivers, he has isolated more clearly than anyone before him a structural point of view in absolute contrast with the substantialist tendency prevailing in Britain. He is the first, one is tempted to say, to have provided anthropology with what it needed: a logical tool for the study of wholes. That he may have let himself be carried away, in the ecstasy of his discoveries, into developments less secure than those which a more systematic and finer use of this tool might have produced is of little importance compared with the fertility of the way which has been opened up. This fertility will be demonstrated by what remains to be discussed, namely the critical development of the theory in the hands of its adherents.

H. AFTER *ELEMENTARY STRUCTURES*

In order to centre attention on the main points, it seems useful to summarize all that has followed from *Elementary Structures* under just three headings, which will be subdivided as required.

30. Local and Global Points of View

A mere two years after the appearance of *Elementary Structures*, Edmund R. Leach published a long article which came across as a violent critique bearing the stamp of hostility, but which in reality was nothing less than the introduction of Lévi-Straussian structuralism into England by a follower who is certainly original and independent, but on the whole very shrewd ('The Structural Implications of Matrilateral Cross-Cousin Marriage', *Journal of the Royal Anthropological Institute*, Vol. LXXXI, 1951, pp. 23–53, cited hereafter as *Rethinking Anthropology*, Ch. 3). No doubt this conversion was to some extent foreshadowed in Leach's earlier work, witness his article on the Jinghpaw terminology, from which I quote this paragraph here as an indication of everything that will follow:

> I suggest that the kinship terminology bears a specific relationship to an idealized form of the social order, but that there is no such obvious relationship between the kinship terminology and the social order as manifested in actual behaviour. (*Rethinking Anthropology*, p. 51)

Here we see Radcliffe-Brown's thesis, modified in a way which prefigures to some extent the very conclusions we are going to reach.

It is no less true that in the person of Leach, and from his first contribution on the question, the heritage of Radcliffe-Brown – to say nothing of Malinowski – comes into contact with structuralism: Anglo-Saxon empiricism came to discuss, perhaps sometimes to misunderstand, but usefully to control, the fruits of French intellectualism.

I shall leave aside many things in Leach's article: his criticisms, whether justified or not, of the ethnographic inaccuracies and speculative transports of his model, his sometimes debatable reconstructions of the history of ideas on the question, his comparative considerations. I shall limit myself to the essentials: the criticism of Lévi-Strauss's theses and procedures, both in general and, better still, as regards the Kachin, of whom Leach had direct experience. To the first belongs the criticism of his diagrams, such as those we have used above in passing from the local to the global point of view. To the second belong criticisms of the supposed implications that Lévi-Strauss draws at the outset concerning one sort of matrilateral intermarriage, first as regards the difference of status between 'exchange' units, second as regards the idea that such a formula – which is by definition local – implies the existence of one or several intermarrying circles or cycles of exchange at a global level.

(a) Exogamous Unit and 'Exchange' Unit

Right at the start, Leach asks us to distinguish between what he calls a 'descent line' and a 'local line'. The first, *ligne d'unifiliation* in French, is what we plot on our diagrams when we wish to represent a form of intermarriage. The second, the 'local line', is the line observed in reality, 'locally'. We should perhaps rather say 'diagrammatic line', or theoretical line, and concrete line. In any case, we have opposed 'local' to global in a totally different sense. For Leach, the word 'local' refers also to 'local descent group', i.e. to that part of a descent group which, from the fact that it resides in the same place, is liable to act collectively, as a more or less 'corporate' group. In fact, he declares categorically that it is the members of such a group who actually arrange marriages. It has to be understood that the real or empirical unit of intermarriage or 'exchange' is neither an individual nor a group corresponding to our diagrammatic 'line', nor the exogamous unit, the whole descent group, as Lévi-Strauss tended to suppose – perhaps, as Leach thinks, because he passed without realising it from his diagrammatic line to the whole exogamous group, perhaps because the simplest supposition on the matter is that the exogamous group and unit of intermarriage coincide. There are in reality two surreptitious moves that Leach is guarding against, one from diagram to reality, from diagrammatic line to real unilineal group – one is thus drawn into reading the partial, or as I would say local diagram in the manner of a global diagram – and the other from exogamous unit to exchange unit. On this last point, there is no need to subscribe to Leach's slightly dogmatic declaration, for marriages can be arranged between smaller groups, for example, between families: it is sufficient to admit that the 'exchange' unit is generally smaller than the exogamous unit (in the sense of the largest group which can be called exogamous).

This point has been abundantly corroborated by Needham, who distinguishes in the same way between descent group and alliance group (Sumba, bibliog. no. 18a, p. 176, etc.; Purum, bibliog. no. 18b, p. 85, etc.), and by myself in my, as it were, experimental test of structuralist theses in south India (*Sous-caste*, 1957, p. 193). The point is obviously very important from the point of view of the passage from the local properties of a definite form of intermarriage to its global properties. In the first place, it can lead to the blurring of the contrast between different forms, or more exactly to complex formulas in which the different forms called restricted exchange and generalised exchange are combined. There may indeed by two exogamous units, A and B, between which reciprocal marriages are postulated. If the unit of intermarriage is a segment of the exogamous unit, intermarriage will take place between a segment An of A and a segment Bp of B, and one can imagine that, at this level, intermarriage may no longer be reciprocal, but oriented, i.e. that A1 gives to B1, who gives to A2, who gives to B2, etc. One would then have, as in the case of the Aimol – such, at least, as reconstituted by Needham (Aimol, bibliog. no. 18d, Fig. 1, p. 94) – asymmetry at the local or 'real' level, but symmetry at the global or ideological level. Or again, the segments A1, A2, A3 of an exogamous group A can be in symmetric marriage relations with segments of different exogamous groups, respectively B1, C2, D3, for example. We might even suppose that such a dispersal will be observed whenever it is not prevented by a global marriage rule present in the consciousness of those involved, as in Australia. Finally, the statement has a very particular impact on the simplest and most spectacular global consequence attributable to asymmetric or oriented alliance: marriage in a circle.

(b) Intermarriage in a Circle

It is known that this idea does not date from *Elementary Structures*. I have mentioned the 'circulating connubium' of Dutch scholars studying Indonesian populations. In his study of the Purum, Needham was able to take into account, and base himself upon, the monograph of an Indian, T.C. Das, which dates from 1945. Needham, while recognising that intermarriage took place between lineages, not clans, tried to save the idea of 'cycles of connubium' by multiplying them. He gives twenty different 'examples' of them. We might wonder whether, at this point, the idea does not lose all value, for it is always possible – provided one has sufficiently copious genealogies at one's disposal and provided the matrilateral rule is sufficiently well followed – to retrace, more or less arbitrarily, chains which, going from one marriage to another, come to an end at a certain moment by closing themselves through returning to their point of departure. The very number that can be constructed bears witness to the gratuitousness of the process, and, as has rightly been observed (J. Berting and H. Philipsen, *Bijdragen*, Vol. 116, 1960, p. 58), in order to preserve the idea of cycles, they must be limited in number and present in the consciousness of those involved. It is in vain for Lévi-Strauss to retort again recently that a bicycle whose handlebars are tilted to one side will necessarily cut back on its tracks, for this is once again to confuse the local and the global points of view. There is no circulating subject, and each 'exchange' unit can see a circle closing in on itself. One cannot draw a holistic formula from a local rule.

Here again, Leach's criticism (*Rethinking Anthropology*, pp. 73, 79) has been decisive. He has declared war on the idea of 'marriage circles', seeing in it an observer's reification of ideal representations, which has certainly been the case to some extent, notably as regards the tribes of the confines of India studied by Indians. Above all, arming himself with the Kachin example, he showed how Lévi-Strauss's antinomy between the difference of status which accompanies the system and the necessity of forming a circle is actually dissolved.

(c) Oriented Intermarriage and 'Hypergamy'

The Kachin offer a good example of matrilateral marriage or 'generalised exchange' (see Fig. 5 above, §26). Lévi-Strauss devoted two chapters (XV and XVI) of his book to them, and Leach, who had worked among them, did not restrict himself to criticism of these chapters but offered, in the article already cited, his own analysis of their system. Lévi-Strauss replied at length to Leach's criticisms (1967 edn., pp. 272–80/235–42), but only to maintain his own theses intact and to limit himself to certain alterations of detail. In the final analysis, and on the main point, where are we now?[16]

Lévi-Strauss, finding very marked differences of rank or status among the Kachin, has been able to bring these facts into relation with their rule of asymmetric marriage and their distinction between *mayu* and *dama*, wife-givers and wife-takers. What was the direction, or meaning, of this difference? Who, wife-takers or wife-givers, were superior, and who inferior? The author did not reply directly to this question, but for reasons given by Leach (p. 80) and for other reasons that can be inferred, not only from Lévi-Strauss's arguments (p. 324/265–66) but also from the general orientation of the book, the reader is led to see the 'wife-takers' as superior to the 'wife-givers'. Now Leach shows that it is

---

[16] The reader may find, here and elsewhere, that I have moved away excessively from the letter of *Elementary Structures*, but nothing else was possible. Stating, in the Preface to the 1967 edition, that 'he should have rewritten it entirely' (p. xiv/xxvii), the author declined to bring it up to date; he has thus left us in charge of it, as it were. On the point which detains us here, any reader who would like to carry out a precise examination of the two Kachin chapters in the two editions of *Elementary Structures* and of Leach's text – an excellent exercise – would no doubt agree with us and understand in particular why I may have neglected the main theme of the second chapter.

the opposite. What is the impact of this fact? The question of the general theory of 'hypergamy' in *Elementary Structures* (India and China) must be left aside here. There remains: 1) the fact that the status difference, not necessarily being in the direction expected or conforming to the 'most frequent type' (p. 336/***), can be conceived at the limit not to exist – in other words, matrilateral marriage would accommodate itself very well to a difference in status, but this would not result from it 'almost unavoidably' (p. 325/266–67); 2) the idea, in itself summary and unexpected, that women are the most precious objects of exchange (Ch. V, pp. 78, 80, 84/60–66) is directly contradicted.

Lévi-Strauss thought that matrilateral marriage or generalised exchange carried within it the seeds of its own destruction, for, while it presupposed equality between exchange units, it produced inequality between them, which logically had to involve its rupture (p. 325/266). Now Leach shows the system as functioning both between superiors and inferiors and between equals (Fig. 9), the difference in status resulting from it being little marked or neutralised in the second case. Above all, Leach insists, the circulation really only 'closes' if one takes into account, not only women, but the totality of prestations exchanged, including non-material goods: the powerful in fact redistribute, for prestige reasons, goods – livestock – which otherwise would accumulate in their hands. In short, things are much more complex than was abstractly supposed to begin with, and the system is much more supple in its actual working. This is so because: (1) the exchange units are smaller than the exogamous units or clans;[17] (2) the status difference is flexible and combines with differences from other sources; (3) it is the totality of prestations that forms a whole, not the simple exchange of women. Moreover, Lévi-Strauss supposed this to be the case in principle, following Mauss, at least in Ch. 5 (see the quotations

---

[17] Lévi-Strauss explicitly recognises that intermarriage functions 'at all levels' (p. 309/253), but in his argument he accords a primacy to intermarriage between the five 'principal' or, as I would say, maximal groups.

[18] At first sight there is a striking discontinuity here. Thus the complex diagram of Tikopia exchanges given on pages 83/64 is not considered to be 'pathological', as is the case for that of the Haka Chin. What renders the latter 'pathological' in the mind of the author is the contradiction between is complexity and the supposed simplicity corresponding to the matrimonial rule. This supposes an idea which is, I believe, not expressed at all, i.e. that 'elementary strcutures' are normally accompanied only by prestations that are simple and reduced: in other words, wherever the exchange of women is directly regulated, other exchanges are not developed. (The interpretation of Bantu *lobola* or 'brideprice' (p. 577/466–67) leans in the same direction.) Such a proposition would need to be established as fact. To the extent that it is not, it supports Leach's accusation that Lévi-Strauss arbitrarily isolated (and, contrary, let us add, to his own Ch. V) the domain of kinship from other domains as regards the exchanges. Leach himself, careful to preserve an empirical significance for the word 'exchange', introduces a different relation (which he attributes, wrongly, to Lévi-Strauss): for him, in 'restricted exchange' women are exchanged against women, while in 'generalised exchange' women are exchanged against goods (p. 79, §d, ii–iii).

above, §22), though it seems to have been somewhat lost from view in the chapters on the Kachin and elsewhere.[18]

To return to the general theory, in ruling out or greatly complicating the passage from the local point of view (rule of individual marriage) to the global point of view (means of integrating the groups constituting the society), it might seem that to retain the criticisms and changes we have just accepted is to return to removing all general interest from the study of types of intermarriage. We shall see below how another, even more radical criticism comes in its turn to modify the picture completely in this respect.

31. Prescription and Preference: Patrilateral Marriage

There is in *Elementary Structures* one rather ambiguous aspect that Needham has sought to clarify. The diagrams suppose that all actual marriages conform to the rule. But this is not so. There is no difficulty here for Lévi-Strauss, for he distinguishes, certainly with good reason, between the normative aspect and the statistical aspect. At least in the domain of representations, the matter is perfectly clear: people's conceptions are linked to an ideal form which they have of their kinship system. Practice can differ quite considerably from this model without affecting it precisely because, to the very extent that it does differ, it is, if not condemned, at any rate considered devoid of meaning. This does not mean that there is no interest for the observer in the extent to which marriages actually conform to the norm, or even, if it were ever possible, in the point from which the quantity (of non-conformity) is changed into quality (change of norm).

But there are related questions that are no less irritating. Lévi-Strauss speaks indifferently, in respect of marriage rules, of prescription and of preference: should we not think that it is necessary to distinguish them, and that preference cannot have exactly the same effects, or the same concomitants, as prescription? This is not unrelated to the more or less precise definition of the spouse: it can be supposed that there can only be prescription wherever the definition is sufficiently broad to ensure the probable existence of a potential spouse. Only if the definition were a narrow one, for example, if it were a case – let us suppose for a moment – of the sole own daughter of one's actual mother's brother, would the rule have to content itself with being a preferential one at the cost of being infringed too often through the non-existence of such a person who is of suitable age. We have noted above the distinction between the definition of the potential spouse by dividing the whole society into matrimonial classes (moieties, etc.), i.e. through a global process, and its definition by tracing individual relationships of kinship, i.e. through a local process. But, at the same level as these latter, it is still necessary in any case to distinguish between class and individual in the usage of the literature or of observers. Indeed, the terminology is *classificatory*, which means that it classifies under the same term many other kinship relations than that corresponding to the actual matrilateral cross cousin, i.e. in principle and very generally all her parallel cousins also (her father's brother's daughters, mother's sister's daughters, etc.). Now the anthropologist himself very often tends to think in individual terms, not classificatory ones, and, if he translates the indigenous term as 'mother's brother's daughter', it would be rare, considering all the literature, for him to have recorded sufficiently precisely what must be understood by it. Thus it is possible to distinguish prescription and preference in the famous Kariera system as described by no less an observer than Radcliffe-Brown: the prescription relates to the category *ñuba*, which contains all the cross cousins of opposite sex to ego, both patrilateral and matrilateral, and which is even broader, since in fact it corresponds to the half-section corresponding to that of the subject in the opposite moiety, there being only four half-sections in a moiety, though we are told at the same time that the first preference is for the mother's brother's daughter (etc.).

This is not all, for, in cases where the rule bears on a relationship of classificatory kinship, we still need to know if there is any other limitation. In effect, if intermarriage is regarded as taking place between exogamous units or their segments, we can expect that only the equivalents of the particular cousin *who fall into the same exogamous group* will be taken into consideration. For example, certain Maravar of South India, who are matrilineal and patrilocal, have such a marked preference for the patrilateral cross cousin that, if the actual cousin is lacking, she must be replaced by an equivalent one, even though distant. Now the genealogies show that this equivalent is nearly always a parallel cousin *in the maternal line* of the former, who thus belongs to the same exogamous group, which has the effect of making the preference bear on one generation of this group (Dumont, *Hierarchy and Marriage Alliance*, p. 41).

Rodney Needham has attacked these questions in a whole series of articles discussing the ethnographic descriptions of several groups, mainly from the point of view of patrilateral marriage (see, above all, bibliog. no. 18c). He has been struck by the difference between the well-known cases of the matrilateral formula and the alleged cases of the patrilateral formula. In the former, it is often easy to define a rigorous prescription and to trace structural concomitants in it. But there is nothing similar in the latter. Needham defines prescription in a complex and draconian manner, more as a characteristic of a certain type of system than as a rule pure and simple. To speak of prescription in effect requires finding united (1) a rule prescribing marriage in respect of certain relationships and forbidding it in respect of others; (2) a corresponding terminological distinction; and even (3) a sufficient degree of application of the rule in practice. There is no doubt that from this point of view there is a difference between matrilateral marriage and patrilateral marriage. In the first case, one encounters, for example, a terminological distinction between the two sorts of cross cousin (point 2) accompanying the rule enjoining marriage with the matrilateral cross cousin and forbidding it with the patrilateral cross cousin (point 1). It certainly seems that nothing comparable is encountered in the patrilateral case, save perhaps exceptionally. But it is a question of knowing whether it is right to formulate the same requirements for both forms of marriage. Indeed, it is very obvious that from its very definition the patrilateral form is more individualising than the matrilateral form: witnesses often characterise it through the deferred return of a woman to the group that has given them one, and this on a small scale, that of the family ('the return of the milk' of central India). In its immediate sense, at least, patrilaterality is characterised by a quick return, not by a long maturation; it does not favour, unlike matrilateral marriage, the creation of permanent units – it is on a small scale. To impose Needham's draconian conditions of prescription upon it may be to declare that only the most robust can carry the burden of doing so, and to blind oneself to the modest manner, though one perhaps well adapted to needs, through which the patrilateral form of intermarriage fulfils its structural or functional purpose. Needham has written that only a 'prescriptive' system has structural implications. To intend this, and for this reason, Lévi-Strauss should have spoken only of prescription, which Lévi-Strauss contests.[19] But we shall see first that there are some more fundamental structural implications, consented to even by Needham, than those which can be detected at the level of relations between social groups. Secondly, must these implications be global to be effective? I have provided a remarkable example of patrilateral marriage in a line of chiefs, insisting on the fact that this form of marriage had allowed, over seven generations, the constitution of a paternal line of succession to the chiefship from only two matrilineal units (there being only matrilineal descent). Apparently this is not a structural implication, since Needham rejects this case as not being prescriptive (in this example there are some cases of matrilateral marriage, but no terminological distinction, though the rule is actually realised here to a totally exceptional degree), and as requiring

---

[19] See here *Elementary Structures*, 1967 edition, pp. xvii–xviii/xxxff. I have profited from certain of the author's arguments here.

further information (*Hierarchy and Marriage Alliance*, Fig. 3, p. 15; cf.
Needham, 'Formal Analysis', pp. 214–15, bibliog. 18c). It is clear that
to limit oneself to prescription in Needham's sense allows a great part
of what actually constitutes 'cross-cousin' marriage to escape in order
to preserve only its most rigid and global aspects.[20]

32. Social Integration and Mental Integration

Lévi-Strauss has seen in intermarriage a privileged form of *relation*.
Anxious to put relation at the very heart of his theory, he generalises
the notion of 'exchange' to the extreme and rests it on that of reciprocity, 'conceived as the most immediate form under which the opposition between myself and others can be integrated' and given as one
of the 'fundamental structures of the mind'. Here again the idea is
strongly generalised: there is mutuality rather than reciprocity in the
model of oriented intermarriage, in which several units give daughters
and receive wives, i.e. the same sort of things, whereas in reciprocity
two units exchange things that may be different (Littre, Dictionnaire).
Likewise, in modern ideology there is no longer reciprocity unless one
places two very different agents opposite one another: myself on one
side, 'the others' on the other, as the formula above and other passages
seem to suggest. At this point the incest prohibition seems like a
requirement of social integration, whereas it can also be taken as the
indelible trace of a distinctive opposition between consanguinity and
marriage, or affinity. As Needham has remarked, in Elementary Structures one passes without transition from relation in the conceptual
sense – distinctive opposition, etc. – to relation empirically speaking, or
reciprocity. The predominant tendency in the book is even, perhaps, to
take reciprocity as the fundamental and irreducible idea. It is on this
point that Needham has gone furthest in his constructive criticism of
the theory when he writes, in one passage of his article on the Aimol:

---

[20] The distinction introduced by Needham, whatever name one chooses to give it, will
nonetheless prove useful in the future, above all, perhaps, in the matter of levels (more immediately than total systems). Thus, in south India again, I doubtless neglected to be more systematic in indicating the hierarchy between the two levels I distinguished: the *imperative* level
of the common (sub-)regional culture with its symmetric aspect, and the *subordinate* level of
a particular group with its particular preference. The matrilaterality of the Pramalai Kallar is
merely one variant on the symmetric base, it is not the 'prescriptive' unilaterality of the
Kachin in Needham's sense (bibliog. no. 19, and *Sous-caste*).

I follow Lévi-Strauss in seeking fundamental features of the human mind as grounds of these systems, but these features are not, I think, mere points of departure, but themselves enclose the principles by which the systems may be explained. In particular, I would reverse his proposition about opposition and reciprocity. The notion of 'exchange', invaluable though it is in the analysis of prescriptive alliance, is a mediating concept. Reciprocity itself, I should maintain, is one modality of opposition; and opposition is manifested in many ideological spheres where there is no question of transfer or exchange. It is this notion of opposition, therefore, which must now engage our attention. (102–3)

It could not be better said, for Lévi-Strauss is not one to claim the primacy of the distinctive opposition. Had he needed to, we read in *The Savage Mind*, in the course of a discussion with Sartre, this precious passage, in which he confesses to a residue of positivism:

I must confess to ... having seemed all too often ... as if I were seeking out an unconscious genesis of matrimonial exchange. [...] I should have made more distinction between exchange ... [matter of praxis, LD] and the conscious ... rules by which these same groups ... spend their time in codifying and controlling it. If there is anything to be learnt from the ethnographic enquiries of the last twenty years, it is that the latter aspect is much more important than has generally been realized by observers who labour under the same delusion as Sartre. (1966 English edition, pp. 251–52 [quotation modified slightly to conform better to the original, RP].)

In other words, there is no explanation for the empirical which does not pass through the ideological. Put another way, the Lévi-Strauss of *Elementary Structures* is in the last resort pre-structuralist. Moreover, to say 'rules' is to say 'concepts', and even where we do not manage to find a global form of intermarriage, we can be assured of coming face to face with a global form of the conception of kinship. Lévi-Strauss has said about totemism, most happily, that beyond what is 'good to eat' there is what is 'good to think'. It is here, at the level of the conceptual universe of kinship, at the level of terminology in particular and, from the point of view of method, at the level of the distinctive opposition that we run aground. It will be objected that perhaps this is not true in every case: are there not systems that have changed or that are 'not very systematic'? Doubtless, but in the domain we are concerned with we will really find very little of this, once adaptations of method are assured. In theory, at any rate, we thus find at the level of the integration of ideas in the mind what seemed to have escaped us at the level of the integration of groups in the society.

And it is here that Needham's distinction between prescription and preference loses much of its force, for preference also has structural implications at this level. Let us take the example of the Pramalai Kallar (in south India), who can be called prescriptive for their marriage of cross cousins in general, preferential for their predilection for the matrilateral cousin. It is true that the matrilateral preference has none of the expected implications at the level of groups (neither significant cycles of intermarriage, nor differences of rank, although the difference between wife-givers and wife-takers is very clearly conceptualised). The real function of these rules turns around an ideal formulation, more or less realised in fact, of the role of the maternal uncle as identical to the father-in-law (of a man), a role concerning prestations and ceremonies which dramatically opposes him to the father, in conformity with the Tamils' predilection for sharp and stylised oppositions. The rule thus works to model a reality lived in conformity with a formula of order, of honour and, we may say, of beauty, which is present in the mind. Should it be thought nothing to have given the ages of life the form of a sort of ballet, the most sumptuous possible, indeed, but above all rigorously in conformity with the imperious order of human relations, since it results in the complementarity of opposites and emerges in the apotheosis of the relation? In this sense we can say, with Lévi-Strauss, that such a rule, though it may appear preferential at the level of observation, is very much prescriptive at the level of the indigenous model ('The Future of Kinship Studies', p. 17).

Marriage rules therefore have structural implications infinitely broader than the mere arrangement of groups. As opposed to expressions based on exchange, etc., the expression 'marriage alliance' can cover simultaneously the general aspect of mental implications and the particular aspect of the implications of social morphology. One may either restrict it to cases in which the definition of the spouse is given exclusively in individual or 'local' terms (cousin marriage in the proper sense), or extend it to cases in which it includes a global formula of intermarriage (Australian sections). The expression suggests above all – and this is important from the conceptual point of view, as well as for its morphological implications – that affinity is something not only collective but permanent in these systems, something which is inherited or transmitted from one generation to another, just as we are accustomed to thinking of consanguinity alone. The rules concerning the topic to which we apply the jargonistic expression 'cross cousin' are all aimed at this transmission of affinity under one form or another. The essence of these systems is that, while for us affinity is something ephemeral which is ultimately encompassed by consanguinity, for them, on the contrary, it is a permanent and important aspect, and in the case of symmetric systems, at least, an exact counterpoint of consanguinity.

This is not a figment of the imagination or a literary formula: it is the means by which we can, starting from our own conceptions, truly understand very different institutions – can compare, in short, two very different sorts of whole or system.

Although the process of discovery is not at an end, with much progress remaining to be made, notably in the study of the terminologies, there are many other types of system that we cannot compare in this way. Let us nonetheless observe that, in passing from the semi-empirical theory of exchange to a theory which is above all conceptual, we are generalising our perspective and opening the way to the study of systems which cannot be said to be based on exchange. Every kinship system will harness the general or elementary ideas we know in one way or another: descent, siblingship, marriage and affinity, transmission, succession, inheritance. Even in the case of cognatic systems, if – as might be thought, and as Lévi-Strauss has suggested (*Annuaire du Collège de France*, 1962, p. 212) – the exercise of rights over the soil is inseparable from what appears elsewhere as kinship in the proper sense, there is nothing wrong in striving to construct a system in which they appear, in one form or another, in combination with what seem elsewhere to be the elements of kinship.

BASIC BIBLIOGRAPHY

(references listed in order of their appearance in the text)

Part I

1. *Notes and Queries on Anthropology*, 6th edition, London: Royal Anthropological Institute 1951.
2. A.R. Radcliffe-Brown, *Structure and Function in Primitive Society*, London: Cohen and West 1952 (especially 'The Study of Kinship Systems', pp. 49–89).
3. A.R. Radcliffe-Brown and Daryll Forde (eds), *African Systems of Kinship and Marriage*, Oxford: Oxford University Press 1950 (especially 'Introduction' by Radcliffe-Brown, pp. 1–85).
4. John Beattie–David Schneider controversy, *Man* 1964, articles 130, 217 (references to Gellner, Needham, Barnes), *Man* 1965, articles 38, 108, 109.
5. Claude Lévi-Strauss, 'L'analyse structurale en linguistique et en anthropologie in his *Anthropologie structurale*, Paris: Plon 1958, pp. 37–62 (translated as 'Structural Analysis in Linguistics and in Anthropology', in his *Structural Anthropology*, London: Allen Lane 1968, pp. 31–54).

Part II

6a. W.H.R. Rivers, 'Mother-Right', *Encyclopaedia of Religion and Ethics*, 1915, Vol. 8, p. 851a.
6b. W.H.R. Rivers, *Social Organization*, London: Kegan Paul, Trench, Trubner & Co. 1926, pp. 85–87.
7. E.R. Leach, 'On Certain Unconsidered Aspects of Double Descent Systems', *Man* 1962, article 214 (and Daryll Forde, *Man* 1963, article 9).
8. E.E. Evans-Pritchard, *The Nuer: A Description of the Modes of Livelihood and Political Institutions of a Nilotic People*, Oxford: Clarendon Press 1940.

9. E.E. Evans-Pritchard, *Kinship and Marriage Among the Nuer*, Oxford: Clarendon Press 1951.
10. Meyer Fortes, 'The Structure of Unilineal Descent Groups', *American Anthropologist*, Vol. LV/1, 1953, pp. 17–41.
11. E.R. Leach–Meyer Fortes controversy, *Man* 1957, article 59; 1959, articles 309, 331; 1960, article 6.
12. Jack Goody, 'The Classification of Double Descent Systems', *Current Anthropology*, Vol. II/1, 1961, pp. 3–25 (text and collective discussion).
13. Jack Goody, 'The Mother's Brother and the Sister's Son in West Africa', *Journal of the Royal Anthropological Institute*, Vol. LXXXIX/1, 1959, pp. 61–88.

Part III

14. Claude Lévi-Strauss, *Les structures élémentaires de la parenté*, Paris: Presses Universitaires Françaises 1949 (2nd edn. 1967; translated as *The Elementary Structures of Kinship*, Boston: Beacon Press 1969).
15. E.R. Leach, *Rethinking Anthropology*, London: The Athlone Press 1961 (especially Ch. 3, pp. 54–104).
16. R. Needham, *Structure and Sentiment: A Test Case in Social Anthropology*, Chicago: The University of Chicago Press 1962.
17. D. Maybury-Lewis, 'Prescriptive Marriage Systems', *Southwestern Journal of Anthropology*, Vol. XXI/3, 1965, pp. 207–30.
18. R. Needham:
    a) 'Circulating Connubium in Eastern Sumba', *Bijdragen tot de Taal-, Land- en Volkenkunde*, Vol. 113, 1957, pp. 168–78.
    b) 'A Structuralist Analysis of Purum Society', *American Anthropologist*, Vol. LX/1, 1958, pp. 75–101.
    c) 'The Formal Analysis of Prescriptive Patrilateral Cross-Cousin Marriage', *Southwestern Journal of Anthropology*, Vol. XIV/2, 1958, pp. 199–219.
    d) 'A Structural Analysis of Aimol Society', *Bijdragen tot de Taal, Land- en Volkenkunde*, Vol. 116, 1960, pp. 81–108.
19. L. Dumont, *Hierarchy and Marriage Alliance in South Indian Kinship*, London: Royal Anthropological Institute, Occasional Papers no. 12, 1957.

Other References in Text

(listed in order of their appearance)

Part I

Lewis Henry Morgan, *Systems of Consanguinity and Affinity of the Human Family*, Washington: Smithsonian Institution 1871.

E.E. Evans-Pritchard, *Essays in Social Anthropology*, London: Faber and Faber 1962 ('Social Anthropology, Past and Present', pp. 13–28).

Marcel Mauss, *Manuel d'ethnographie*, Paris: Payot 1947.

C.N. Starcke, *The Primitive Family*, London: Kegan Paul 1889.

Meyer Fortes, 'Radcliffe-Brown's Contributions to the Study of Social Organization', *British Journal of Sociology*, Vol. VI, 1955, pp. 16–30.

A.R. Radcliffe-Brown–L. Dumont controversy ('Dravidian Kinship Terminology'), *Man* 1953, articles 54, 169.

Part II

Louis Dumont, *La civilisation indienne et nous*, Paris: A. Colin 1964.

Louis Dumont, *Homo Hierarchicus*, Paris: Gallimard 1966 (translation, London: Weidenfeld & Nicolson 1970, The University of Chicago Press 1980).

Louis Dumont, 'The Modern Conception of the Individual: Notes on its Genesis', *Contributions to Indian Sociology*, Vol. VIII, 1965, pp. 13–61.

Michel Villey, 'La Formation de la pensée juridique moderne: Le Franciscanisme et le droit', Paris: Les Cours de Droit 1963 (mimeo).

'Esquisse d'un glossaire de la parenté', *L'Échange*, no. 7, May 1966.

David Pocock, *Social Anthropology*, London: Sheed and Ward 1961.

Louis Dumont, Preface to E.E. Evans-Pritchard, *Les Nuer*, Paris: Gallimard 1968 (translated in *Essays in Memory of E.E. Evans-Pritchard by his Former Oxford Colleagues*, (ed.) J. Beattie and R.G. Lienhardt, Oxford: Clarendon Press 1975).

E.E. Evans-Pritchard, *Witchcraft, Oracles and Magic Among the Azande*, Oxford: Clarendon Press 1937.

M.G. Smith, 'Segmentary Lineage Systems', *Journal of the Royal Anthropological Institute*, Vol. LXXXVI/2, 1956, pp. 39–80.

Marshall D. Sahlins, 'The Segmentary Lineage: An Organization of Predatory Expansion', *American Anthropologist*, Vol. LXIII, 1961, pp. 322–45.

David M. Schneider, 'Double Descent on Yap', *Journal of the Polynesian Society*, Vol. LXXI/1, 1962, pp. 1–24.

Louis Dumont, 'Marriage in India: The Present State of the Question, Part 1', *Contributions to Indian Sociology*, Vol. V, 1961, pp. 75–95.

Part III

G.C. Homans and D.M. Schneider, *Marriage, Authority, and Final Causes: A Study of Unilateral Cross-Cousin Marriage*, Glencoe: Free Press 1955.

Louis Dumont, 'Descent or Intermarriage? A Relational View of Australian Section Systems', *Southwestern Journal of Anthropology*, Vol. XXII/3, 1966, pp. 231–50.

R.F. Fortune, 'A Note on Some Forms of Kinship Structure', *Oceania* IV, 1933, pp. 1–9.

Louis Dumont, 'Sur le vocabulaire de parenté Kariera', in J. Pouillon and P. Maranda (eds), *Échanges et Communications Mélanges offerts à Claude Lévi-Strauss*, Paris and The Hague: Mouton 1970, pp. 272–86.

Louis Dumont, *Une sous-caste de l'Inde du Sud: Organisation sociale et religion des Pramalai Kallar*, Paris and The Hague: Mouton 1957.

T.C. Das, *The Purums: An Old Kuki Tribe of Manipur*, Calcutta: University of Calcutta 1945.

J. Berting and H. Philipsen, 'Solidarity, Stratification and Sentiments: The Unilateral Cross-Cousin Marriage According to the Theories of Lévi-Strauss, Leach, and Homans and Schneider', *Bijdragen tot de Taal-, Land- en Volkenkunde*, Vol. 116, 1960, pp. 55–80.

Claude Lévi-Strauss, *La pensée sauvage*, Paris: Plon 1962 (English translation, *The Savage Mind*, London: Weidenfeld & Nicolson 1966).

Claude Lévi-Strauss, 'The Future of Kinship Studies', *Proceedings of the Royal Anthropological Institute*, 1965, pp. 13–22.

Claude Lévi-Strauss, 'Anthropologie sociale', *Annuaire du Collège de France*, 1962, p. 212.

INDEX